Vengeance Weapon 2

The V-2 Guided Missile

Gregory P. Kennedy

Published for
the National Air and Space Musuem

by

the Smithsonian Institution Press

Washington, D.C. 1983

Library of Congress Cataloging in Publication Data

Kennedy, Gregory P., 1940–
Vengeance weapon 2.
Bibliography: p.
Supt. of Docs. no.: SI 9.2:W37
1. V–2 rocket. I. Title.
UG1282.G8K46   1983   623.4′543′0943   82–600400

ISBN 0-87474-573-X

Ta

A Bronx Cheer in Smoke   **4**
The Wehrmacht Begins Building Rockets   **6**
Peenemünde   **12**
A-4   **16**
Mass Production   **22**
Field Deployment Preparations   **30**
V-2   **35**
The V-2 at War   **38**
Reaping the Harvest   **52**

Appendix 1.   **68**
   A Technical Description of the A-4.
   a.   *Warhead*   **68**
   b.   *Control Compartment*   **70**
   c.   *Midsection*   **74**
   d.   *Propulsion Section*   **76**
   e.   *Tail Unit*   **78**
Appendix 2.   **81**
   The V-2 in the National Air and Space Museum
Appendix 3.   **84**
   The A-4 Missile Statistics

Bibliography   **84**

A Bronx Cheer in Smoke

Close-up of a V-2 in flight (S.I. Negative #79-6557).

ON 29 OCTOBER 1944, Lieutenants Donald A. Schultz and Charles M. Crane of the United States 7th Photo Reconnaissance Group were dispatched on a sortie that included Mannheim, Ludwigshafen, and Schweinfurt. The weather report was good—cloud cover over their targets was between two-tenths and five-tenths. Compared to the weather of the past few days (which had kept most of the group grounded), it was almost as good as flying under unlimited-visibility conditions.

Shortly after the pilots crossed the Rhine River a cigar-shaped projectile popped up out of the trees a few hundred yards in front of them. They clearly saw the 30-foot flame issuing from the projectile's base and the gray-white vapor trail it left behind. As the object came closer, it became obvious that it was not one of the V-1 Buzz Bombs that had been used against London during the last four months. Crane also ruled out the possibility that it was a jet aircraft. This left one possibility—the projectile was a V-2 rocket, the most recent of Germany's wonder weapons to be committed to war.

Crane decided to try to photograph the missile and dove to intercept it. The missile was accelerating quickly, so he only had a few seconds to take his photographs. While he radioed a description of the object to his wingman Schultz, Crane managed to snap off three exposures with his P-38's nose camera. Crane said he could see the missile very clearly—it was about 45 feet long and 15 feet across at its base. The rocket was moving quite fast by the time it passed the aircraft, and the pilots were quickly left behind.

When the film from Crane's aircraft was developed, he discovered that he had failed to capture the rocket on film. All Crane had caught was the missile's exhaust, which he later described in a BBC interview with American correspondent Chester Morrison as "a Bronx cheer in smoke."

The object sighted by Crane and Schultz was, as they suspected, a German V-2 guided missile. Between 6 September 1944 and 28 March 1945, more than 3000 of the missiles were launched against targets in England and on the Continent. This weapon, the world's first large ballistic missile, more than doubled the range of the fabled Paris Gun of World War I, which many had seen as the ultimate artillery weapon. It carried a one-ton warhead, and it also represented a quantum leap in rocket

Lieutenant Donald A. Schultz, who witnessed a V-2 launch on 29 October 1944, watches as a cassette of film is removed from the nose camera of his P-38 reconnaissance aircraft (U.S. Air Force Photo).

technology. With the advent of the V-2, the liquid-fuel rocket was transformed from a temperamental device capable of delivering a few hundred pounds of thrust to a 25-ton thrust propulsion unit that could be mass produced. In addition to advances made in the area of rocket-motor design and construction, the V-2 spurred developments in such areas as guidance and control and high-speed aerodynamics.

Consider the effort required to field this weapon. First known as the Aggregat-4 (Assembly-4)[1] to the engineers who built it, the missile represented 14 years of work before it was committed to battle. When it was deployed, the war was already lost. Each day, waves of bombers flew over the heart of the "Thousand Year Reich" virtually unchallenged, reducing more and more of Germany's cities to rubble. The Russians advanced relentlessly from the east, while the Western Allies gained ground in Western Europe. German industry lay in ruins and her armed forces had to cope with chronic short-

ages of men and materiel. Despite the dismal military situation on all fronts, Germany continued to develop and deploy new weapons. During the last months of the war, jet- and rocket-powered aircraft, cruise missiles, and long-range guided missiles were introduced. These weapons, however, were deployed in insufficient numbers and much too late in the war to be effective.

Following World War II more than 100 of Germany's top rocket experts emigrated to the United States, where they continued their work. Along with the American scientists and engineers who were launching captured V-2s in the New Mexico desert, they helped lay the foundation for future rocket programs that eventually resulted in the mammoth Saturn V Moon rocket.

1. V-2 stands for Vengeance Weapon-2 (Vergeltungswaffe zwei). This name was proposed by the Nazi propaganda ministry to identify its use as a terror weapon for reprisal against the Allies.

The Wehrmacht Begins Building Rockets

Major General Walter Dornberger, who directed the development of large ballistic missiles in Germany from 1930 to 1945 (S.I. Negative #A5347A).

GERMAN NEWSPAPERS IN THE LATE 1920s carried headlines and stories about rocket builders such as Max Valier who, with the aid of industrialist Fritz von Opel, conducted numerous tests using rockets as a source of power for a variety of vehicles. These tests, which were spectacular if not scientific, were intended to draw public attention to the possibilities of rocketry and space travel. Public interest in these topics was high, and in the summer of 1927 the Verein für Raumschifffahrt (VfR), or Society for Space Travel, was formed as a popular organization to raise money for rocket experiments. By late 1929 the organization had over 1000 members.

The VfR obtained a lease on a tract of land outside Berlin and experimental work at the Raketenflugplatz (literally "Rocket Flying Place") began in 1930. It was also during 1930 that an 18-year-old engineering student named Wernher von Braun joined the group.

Civilian experimenters were not the only people interested in rockets. On 17 December 1930, officers of the German Army's Ordnance Department met to discuss the possibilities of using rockets as weapons. The Versailles Treaty, which ended World War I, imposed severe limitations on the manpower and weaponry of the German forces, but made no mention of rockets; so the Wehrmacht saw rocket development as a legal pursuit under the terms of the settlement. The attendees agreed to pursue the development of rockets, to equip the Kummersdorf Artillery Range 17 miles south of Berlin for rocket trials, and to appoint a technically qualified officer to oversee the program. The officer appointed was Captain Walter R. Dornberger, who had recently received his engineering degree from the Technische Hochschule Charlottenburg, a technical university in Berlin. Dornberger was directed "to develop in military facilities a liquid-fuel rocket, the range of which should surpass that of any existing gun and production for which would be carried out by industry. Secrecy of the development is paramount."[1]

Efforts over the next two years to interest German industry in liquid-fuel rockets were unsuccessful, so Dornberger had to resort to contacting individual experimenters. In the spring of 1932, Captain Dornberger, along with his immediate supervisor Captain Ritter von Horstig and Colonel Karl Becker, head of the Ballistics and Munitions

Rudolf Nebel (left) and a youthful Wernher von Braun (right) at the VfR's experimental center near Berlin, the Raketenflugplatz, ca. 1931 (S.I. Negative #76-7559).

Branch of the Ordnance Department, visited the Raketenflugplatz. They were shown several rockets, but what the visitors from the Ordnance Department wanted to see were technical data regarding the liquid-fuel rockets tested by the VfR. The data did not exist because the VfR's experiments were directed toward building a working rocket that could be used as a demonstration device to help solicit funds for more research.

In July a group from the VfR traveled to Dornberger's Experimental Station West at Kummersdorf to fly one of their rockets for the Army. The rocket attained an altitude of only 200 feet. Based on what they saw at the Raketenflugplatz and Kummersdorf, the officers of the Ordnance Department decided that the rocket was unpredictable at best, and that too much showmanship and not enough engineering had gone into the VfR's efforts. Rockets did offer sufficient promise, however, to warrant further work. Also, Dornberger noticed the youthful von Braun's work and offered him a civilian position at Kummersdorf.

On 1 November 1932, von Braun reported for work at

Experimental Station West, where his first task was to build a 650-pound thrust liquid-fuel rocket motor. The motor, which burned liquid oxygen and a mixture of 75 percent ethyl alcohol and 25 percent water, was ready for its first static-firing in late December. A concrete-lined pit with 18-foot thick walls and a sliding wooden roof had been built for testing rocket motors. The static test stand pit was equipped to permit the motor's thrust and propellant consumption rates to be measured.

All was ready for the first static firing on the night of 21 December. Dornberger stood behind a small tree a scant 10 yards from the test stand, shivering in the bitter cold. Von Braun was at the front of the U-shaped testing pit, holding a 12-foot pole with a can of gasoline on its end. Both men studied the 20-inch pear-shaped duralumin motor gleaming in the harsh light of two searchlights. Engineer Walter Riedel and mechanic Heinrich Grünow were behind the back wall of the test stand, monitoring and regulating the pressures in the fuel and oxidizer tanks. Finally Riedel announced that the pres-

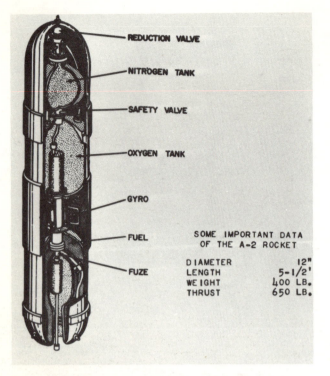

REDUCTION VALVE	
NITROGEN TANK	
SAFETY VALVE	
OXYGEN TANK	
GYRO	
FUEL	
FUZE	

SOME IMPORTANT DATA
OF THE A-2 ROCKET

DIAMETER	12"
LENGTH	5-1/2'
WEIGHT	400 LB.
THRUST	650 LB.

The A-2, first flying liquid-fuel rocket built for the Wehrmacht by Wernher von Braun. Two A-2s, named Max and Moritz, were flown in December 1934 (S.I. Negative #79-12337).

sures in the tanks had reached the desired levels, and von Braun ignited the gasoline on the end of the pole. Riedel opened the propellant valves and a white cloud of oxygen was emitted from the motor's nozzle, followed by a trickle of alcohol. When von Braun moved his improvised taper under the nozzle there was a loud explosion. Bits of metal, cable, and wood flew through the air, some striking the searchlights, which went out. Alcohol and liquid oxygen continued to drip onto the floor and formed puddles, which burned erratically. In the dim light from the burning propellants, Dornberger and von Braun stared at each other. Miraculously the only casualties in the explosion had been the motor and the test stand, which were both destroyed.

Several months later a 650-pound thrust motor was successfully fired on the rebuilt test stand. By mid-1933 this motor was placed in what was intended to be the Kummersdorf group's first flying rocket, the Aggregat-1, (or A-1). For stability, it had a gyroscope with a 70-pound rotor in its forward section. During a static firing the motor exploded, destroying the rocket. It was decided to proceed with the construction of an improved rocket, the A-2, rather than rebuild the shattered A-1. The A-2 was similar to its predecessor—it was the same size and used the same motor. The difference between the two rockets was that the A-2's gyroscope was between the propellant tanks, near the rocket's center of gravity. Two A-2 models were built and prepared for flight in December 1934. The rockets were christened Max and Moritz, after the main characters in the German cartoon strip, which became known as the "Katzenjammer Kids" in America. Both performed perfectly and attained altitudes of about 1.5 miles. With these successes, additional funds for rocket development were allocated by the Army. Work began on an advanced instrument-carrying rocket, the A-3.

In January 1935, Major Wolfram von Richthofen of the Luftwaffe (a cousin of the "Red Baron" of World War I) visited Kummersdorf to investigate the possibilities of using liquid-fuel rockets to power aircraft. The Army did not raise any objections to this so the team at Army Experimental Station West, which had grown to 80 people, began work on the project. By midsummer a 650-pound thrust motor had been installed in a Heinkel 112 aircraft and static tests commenced in the fall. Von Richthofen was so impressed by the quick response to his request that he asked the Kummersdorf group to begin development of a jet-assisted takeoff unit for heavy bombers. When informed that Kummersdorf was too cramped to permit such a project, he offered the group 5,000,000 RM to build adequate facilities at a new location.

The officials in the Army Ordnance Department were upset over the breach of protocol between branches of the Wehrmacht, and responded by allocating 6,000,000 RM for rocket work. Thus, the Wehrmacht's rocket program, which had never before had an annual budget larger than 80,000 marks, suddenly found itself with 11,000,000 RM to dispose of.

Meanwhile, work continued on the A-3. Considerably larger than the A-2, the A-3 used a 3300-pound thrust motor, was 21 feet, 4 inches long, and weighed 1650 pounds at launch. Placing a single, large gyroscope near the rocket's center of gravity was adequate for stabilizing small rockets such as the A-2, but for the A-3 this brute force approach was unsatisfactory. A three-axis gyroscopic control system was designed to guide the A-3. The gyroscopes were coupled with

After the successful A-2 flights a larger rocket, the A-3, was built. Here an A-3 is shown mounted in a static test stand at Kummersdorf Proving Ground (S.I. Negative #77-14790).

Werner Gengelbach, Walter Thiel, and Hans Hueter (left to right), in front of the first successful A-4, flown on 3 October 1942. Dr. Thiel was in charge of propulsion development at Peenemünde. The "Frau im Mond" (woman in the moon) emblem was affixed to the rocket as a decoration. "V4" on the emblem signifies that the rocket was the fourth one built (S.I. Negative #76-13634).

molybdenum vanes placed in the motor's exhaust. Movement of the vanes deflected the exhaust jet and altered the course of the rocket. Kummersdorf was too small to accommodate the A-3, so a new launch site was selected in the Baltic Sea on the island of Greifswalder Oie. The island, which was only 1000 feet long and 300 feet wide, was used only as the launch site; the rocket's flight carried it out over the water.

While the A-3 was being built, the design of the A-4 began to crystallize. Prior to that time the ultimate artillery weapon was the Paris Gun of World War I, which fired a 210 mm shell containing 23 pounds of explosive and had a range of 80 miles. The designers who developed the A-4 sought to double that range and carry a one-ton warhead. The overall length and fin span of the A-4 was determined by the largest size object that could be transported through railroad tunnels and small villages. By mid-1936, the preliminary design for the A-4 was completed; the missile would be about 45 feet long, just over five feet in diameter, and would weigh 12 tons at launch. To deliver a one-ton warhead to a target 160 miles away, the rocket's motor would have to produce a thrust of 25 tons for 60 seconds.

Liquid oxygen and a mixture of 75 percent alcohol, 25 percent water were selected as the oxidizer and fuel, respectively. Ethyl and methyl alcohol were both inexpensive and readily available in large quantities. The water reduced combustion temperature with only a slight loss of engine performance.

Once the parameters for the A-4 were defined, work began on the propulsion unit. In the fall of 1936, Dr. Walter Thiel arrived at Kummersdorf to take charge of propulsion system development. At that time the largest rocket motors in existence delivered thrusts of just over 1.5 tons. The task of trying to obtain complete combustion of the fuel and oxidizer was one of the fundamental obstacles that had to be overcome before a large liquid-fuel rocket motor could be built. In the 1.5-ton motor, propellants were injected under pressure into the combustion chamber in relatively thick streams. Contact between the streams was sufficiently violent to vaporize and mix the liquid oxygen and alcohol. A relatively long combustion chamber (about six feet) was used to maximize the opportunity for an individual droplet of propellant mixture to ignite before reaching the nozzle. What actually happened was that the burning varied in intensity along the length of the combustion chamber, producing areas of heat concentration and causing the motors to burn through.

In an effort to overcome the problems caused by erratic combustion, injection nozzles that atomized the propellants were tried. The new system was successful; propellant burning was more homogeneous and the incidence of burn-throughs decreased. During the next year the combustion chamber was shortened to one foot. Improvements in combustion, however, caused the temperature to rise in the motor, which began to burn through at the nozzle and the brass propellant injectors. These problems were solved by redesigning the nozzle and recessing the propellant-injector head in a cup, removing it from the combustion chamber entirely. The recess also provided a mixing chamber for the alcohol and liquid oxygen before they entered the combustion chamber, further improving combustion.

Dr. Thiel next built a 4.5-ton thrust motor by clustering three of the 1.5-ton unit injector heads. Following the success with a three-head cluster, it was proposed that 18 injector heads be combined to create the 25-ton motor. Experience indicated that hundreds of hours of testing were necessary to fine-tune a large single-injector motor for peak performance, so the expedient of combining 18 smaller injector assemblies was tried. The 18 injector-cup motor worked as planned and delivered a thrust of 25 tons. Dr. Thiel and his staff spent the next several years refining the motor's design, making it a reliable device that could be mass-produced.

In late 1937 four A-3s were ready for flight. As preparations for the first launch took place on the Greifswalder Oie, a feeling of optimism permeated the air. The 3300-pound thrust propulsion unit performed flawlessly during static tests. Dr. Rudolf Hermann validated the aerodynamic stability of the rocket's design in the supersonic wind tunnel at Aachen, and the gyroscopic guidance system was designed by the German Navy's leading expert on gyroscopes, an ex-Austrian Naval officer named Boykow. The rockets were equipped with parachutes so they and their important instrument packages could be recovered.

The first A-3 was ready for launch on 4 December. After a delay of several hours due to mechanical problems (much to the distress of some of the invited dignitaries off-shore in a small boat), the rocket was launched. It lifted off cleanly and rose on course for about five seconds, then arced over unexpectedly. The parachute ejected prematurely and was burned up by the rocket's exhaust. By this time the A-3 was tumbling, and ingloriously ended its out-of-control flight in the deep blue waters of the Baltic. The parachute was removed from the second rocket, for it was suspected that a premature deployment of the recovery system caused the failure of the first flight. The second rocket flight was no better than the first. Rockets three and four also malfunctioned.

The cause for the failures was finally traced to the guidance system. Analysis of the system's performance showed that the corrective force produced by the jet vanes was insufficient to enable the rocket to maintain a straight course in winds of over 12 feet per second. Also, the vanes responded too slowly to changes in the rocket's attitude. This explained the failures of the third and fourth rockets, which were flown in calm weather.

It had been planned to begin construction of the A-4 immediately following the A-3. However, in the absence of a successful A-3 flight, plans for the A-4 were temporarily shelved while the problems encountered with the A-3 were solved. A new test rocket, designated A-5, was built. It used the same motor and was about the same size as the A-3, but the airframe and control system were completely redesigned. The shape of the A-5 was selected based on data from wind tunnel tests for the A-4, so it looked very much like a half-scale model of the larger missile.

Designing and building an adequate guidance system for the A-5 proved to be a more time-consuming task than had been originally estimated, so the first A-5s were flown without the new system. These propulsion and aerodynamic tests were successful, so when the improved guidance system was ready in the autumn of 1939, the A-5 was a flight-qualified vehicle. Among the improvements in the design of the A-5 over that of the A-3 was the use of graphite for the jet vanes instead of molybdenum, reducing the price for a set of vanes from 150 marks to 1.5 marks. When the guidance system was redesigned, the response time for the jet vanes was improved, as was their strength.

Nearly two years after the A-3s tumbled out of control over the Baltic, the first A-5 with its improved guidance system flew successfully. The first two flights of the series were vertical; that is, the gyroscopes were set to maintain a vertical ascent. Both rockets attained altitudes in excess of five miles.

These flights were significant, but one more test was needed to verify the performance of the guidance system; the rocket had to fly a preprogrammed trajectory. On the third flight, the rocket's pitch gyroscope was equipped with a clockwork mechanism that caused it to slowly tilt during the flight. If the control mechanism of the rocket worked properly, the vehicle's longitudinal axis would remain parallel to the axis of the gyroscope, causing the rocket to incline with the gyroscope. After liftoff, A-5 #3 climbed for four seconds. Then, according to plan, the vehicle began to tilt to the east. Finally, the rocket reached the pre-selected 45° angle and continued to accelerate. After reaching an altitude of $2\frac{1}{2}$ miles and a range of four miles, the rocket's parachute deployed. The guidance system performed flawlessly and the flight was a success.

The A-5 continued to be used as a test vehicle for parachute and guidance system tests. About 25 A-5s were flown, some of them several times. In all, approximately 70 flights were made with this test vehicle, which was used until late 1942. After the feelings of anxiety and uncertainty experienced after the A-3 flights, the developers of the A-4 could once again proceed with confidence.

1. Dornberger, Walter. "The Lessons of Peenemünde," Technical Intelligence Branch, OWC, GU-15, 460, undated [ca. 1958].

Peenemünde

As WORK PROGRESSED ON THE A-3 it became obvious that even if launches were conducted from the Greifswalder Oie, Kummersdorf Proving Ground was too small to accommodate a rocket program of even moderate size. After the rocketeers at Experimental Station West received 11,000,000 RM in 1935, one of their first priorities was to find a new location for their research. The first sites examined on the North Sea coast were too close to foreign countries for experiments with long-range rockets to be kept secret. The next proposed site, on the Baltic island of Rugen, seemed ideal. Rockets could be flown from the island for several hundred kilometers over the Baltic Sea. Construction could be easily camouflaged in the existing forests. Rugen, however, with its high white chalk cliffs and other scenic attractions, had already been selected by the leaders of the Kraft durch Freude (strength through joy) movement of the German Labor Front as a resort area, so the Ordnance Department had to continue its search for a rocket research station.

Wernher von Braun was visiting his family during Christmas of 1935 when one of his relatives suggested the island of Usedom, where von Braun's father used to go duck hunting. Usedom is one of two islands that separate the Bay of Stettin and the Baltic Sea. In clear weather it is within visible range of the Greifswalder Oie. The Peene River flows along the western side of the island. A small fishing village, Peenemünde, was located near the river's estuary.

The necessary property was purchased from the City of Wolgast (which owned the island) in April 1936, and work began on the Heers Versuchsstelle Peenemünde (Army Experimental Station Peenemünde), abbreviated HVP. Actually, HVP was a joint services facility with the Army located in the forested area east of Lake Koplin, and the Luftwaffe on the flat northern and western areas of the island. The Army station was designated Peenemünde East, the Luftwaffe Station Peenemünde West.

Construction began under the supervision of the Luftwaffe shortly after the land was purchased. In May 1937 most of the staff (which numbered over 90) of Experimental Station West moved to their new facilities on the Baltic. Test Stand 1, for static tests of large liquid-fuel motors, was not finished, so Dr. Thiel remained at Kummersdorf with a small staff to continue work on the A-4 power plant. (Thiel did not move to

Aerial view of Usedom Island, in the spring of 1944. Numerous small craters are visible near the housing area, the result of previous bombings (S.I. Negative #80-12316).

Peenemünde until 1940.)

Initially, HVP was under the administrative control of an Army Commander, but by 1939 this position was abolished. Thereafter, Peenemündes East and West were maintained as separate entities by their parent services. At about the same time, HVP became HAP, for Heeres Anstalt Peenemünde (Army Establishment Peenemünde).

Development of the A-4 was proceeding, and the facilities at Peenemünde were expanding. While supersonic wind tunnel tests of the A-3 were made by Dr. Rudolf Hermann at Aachen in 1936, von Braun and Dornberger became convinced of the need for a similar facility at Peenemünde. After some salesmanship, Dornberger finally convinced the Army to underwrite the project, which he estimated would cost nearly 1,000,000 RM. Hermann was hired to operate the Army's supersonic wind tunnel and joined the group in the spring of

1937. Many of von Braun's former associates from the VfR were also hired by the Army during the late 1930s.

Despite the support given by the Wehrmacht, the Army's rocket program was initially treated with indifference in the highest levels of the German government. Hitler visited Kummersdorf only once, in March 1939, and never visited Peenemünde. During his visit, he saw cutaway models of the A-3 and A-5 and static firings of several large rocket motors. Throughout his tour, Hitler, who was known for his fascination with new weapons, seemed noncommital and unaffected by what he had seen. To Dornberger, who was accustomed to the enthusiastic reactions shown by people after witnessing the fiery spectacle of a rocket firing, the Führer's lack of emotion seemed strange. The closest thing to a favorable statement made by Hitler during his brief stay at Experimental Station West occurred during lunch. After Dornberger answered

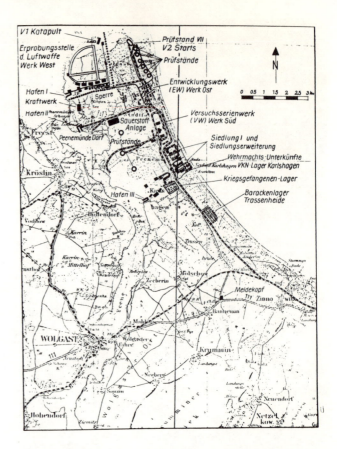

Layout of the Heeres Versuchsstelle Peenemünde (Army Experimental Station Peenemünde) (S.I. Negative #79-12336).

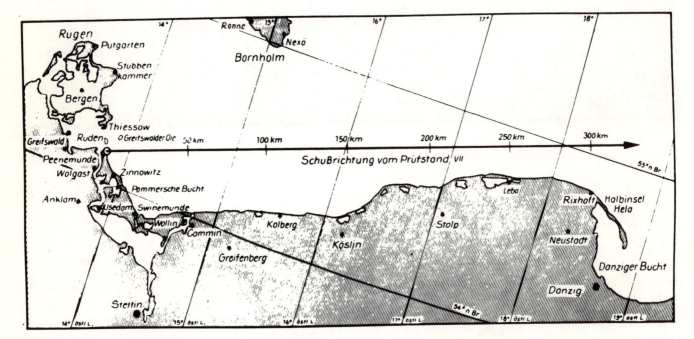

Rockets fired from Peenemünde could fly hundreds of kilometers over the Baltic Sea (S.I. Negative #79-6555).

one of the few questions asked by Hitler, the Führer looked past him with a slight smile and said, "Es war doch gewaltig!", which can be translated as "Well, it was grand!"[1]

The Commander in Chief of the Army, Field Marshall Walther von Brauchitsch, gave the rocket program the highest military priority rating in September 1939. However, by the spring of 1940, following the Wehrmacht's lightning-swift advances across Europe, Hitler removed Peenemünde from the list of military installations authorized to receive national resources. Even worse, many of the center's personnel were being inducted into the Armed Forces.

At this point, the A-4 program would have probably collapsed if not for the intervention of several high-ranking persons. An elaborate ruse was worked out to alleviate the program's personnel shortages. A new unit, the Versuchskommando Nord (VKN, Experimental Command North), was established as a combat unit assigned to the home front at Peenemünde. Inductees who had been scientists, engineers, or technicians in civilian life were transferred from other Army units to the VKN. Materiel shortages were another matter. Funding was barely sufficient to allow work to continue, with no hope of expansion. Facilities were built only because of Albert Speer's personal interest in the A-4. Even prior to his appointment as Minister of Armaments and Munitions on 8 February 1942, Speer supervised many construction projects within the Todt organization and was able to authorize construction of new facilities at Peenemünde despite the station's lack of priority. These ploys certainly aided the missile program and allowed it to survive, but Dornberger realized that additional support was needed if the A-4 was to become a reality. The only way to gain more support was to have the A-4's priority rating elevated. Dornberger was to find securing a high-priority rating for his program a far more difficult task than he first imagined.

1. Dornberger, Walter, *V-2*, p. 66.

A-4

On 3 OCTOBER 1942, AN A-4 STOOD READY for flight on Test Stand VII at Peene-münde. This was the fourth A-4 built, and the third launched. The first A-4 had exploded during a static test. Attempted flights with the second and third rockets on 13 June and 16 August had both ended in failure. After twelve years of work, millions of marks and man-hours, and three spectacular failures, some senior officers in the Wehrmacht were seriously questioning the feasibility of using rockets as long-range artillery weapons. As the fourth vehicle was erected on the launch pad the personnel at Peene-münde realized that a successful flight was crucial to the continuation of the program. Every component of the missile was carefully inspected and tested several times.

Dornberger stood on the roof of the Measurement House. With its covered parapet and unobstructed view of most of the research station, this was an ideal vantage point. Slowly, much too slowly it seemed, the countdown proceeded. Years later, Dornberger recalled how the last few minutes before a launch seemed to last much longer. These became known as "Peenemünde minutes" to those who built and launched the A-4. In the "Peenemünde minutes" on that October day, Dornberger scanned the island. On Test Stand VII, he saw the black and white lacquered rocket, glistening in the sun. Wisps of vapor from the super-cold liquid oxygen exhausted from the vent near the rocket's base. Looking elsewhere, Dornberger saw groups of people scattered about, all focusing on the launch pad. It seemed that everyone associated with the project turned out to observe this critical test. Finally, all was ready and the firing order was given.

"Ignition!" The propulsion engineer in the concrete blockhouse pulled the first of three levers and a shower of sparks rained out of the rocket's base as the igniter functioned. The second was pulled—"Preliminary Stage." During the preliminary stage the motor did not produce enough thrust to lift the $13\frac{1}{2}$-ton vehicle, but did allow the propulsion engineer to observe the rocket's combustion and make sure the propellants were burning properly.

Three seconds later, the third and final lever was pulled. The motor's thrust built up to the full 25 tons and the rocket lifted off.

"Rocket has lifted!" With an initial acceleration of 1 g (about 32 feet per second per second), the A-4 began to climb. Four-and-one-half seconds after liftoff the vehicle

Prelaunch preparations for an A-4 at Test Stand VII, ca. 1943 (S.I. Negative #77-14261).

16

Ignition and lift-off from Test Stand VII. The smoke streamer visible in the upper left corner is from a flare fired just before launch as a warning to personnel on the base (S.I. Negatives #79-12321, #79-12327).

began a preplanned pitch toward the east. As the rocket gained both speed and altitude the pitch program continued until an inclination angle of 50° was reached. After 63 seconds of powered flight, Brennschluss (thrust termination) occurred.

The A-4, its motor silent, coasted like an artillery shell. It continued to climb, reached an altitude of nearly 60 miles, then began the earthward-bound portion of its parabolic trajectory. The rocked impacted in the Baltic Sea 120 miles from Test Stand VII, 296 seconds after lift-off.

There were numerous failures after the success on 3 October 1942, but the engineers and technicians at Peenemünde had demonstrated the potential of the large ballistic missile. When critics of the A-4 program vocalized their doubts, the Ordnance Department could show them sufficient proof to warrant continuing the project. The first successful flight was followed by 23 months of further testing and refining of the missile before it was committed to combat. In that 23-month period Dornberger and his staff had to cope with many technical and political problems.

Dornberger and von Braun met with Speer on 8 January

1943, to appeal for a higher priority rating. A similar request several months earlier resulted in a decision to continue development of the A-4 at its current level, to begin planning for production, and to destroy all but one set of drawings of the missile! This bizarre decree did not alter the A-4's low-priority status nor did it grant any further assistance from the Ministry of Munitions.

Mass production was scheduled to commence by the end of 1943, a goal Dornberger felt was unrealistic if support for the project continued at its current level. After hearing arguments by the men from Peenemünde, Speer replied that Hitler was still skeptical of the A-4, so the project's status remained unchanged.

Speer then announced that Gerhard Degenkolb, previously known as the "Railroad Czar," would be in charge of A-4 production. Speer expressed his confidence that even though he was unable to raise the priority of the rocket program, Degenkolb could accomplish the task of bringing the A-4 to production status.

The A-4 program received yet another blow in early February. After being summoned to the Ministry of Munitions,

Dornberger was informed of a plan whereby the Army experimental station at Peenemünde was to be converted to a private stock company supervised by the Siemans Company. As Professor Karl Hetlage, the official in charge of financial and organizational matters in the armaments industry, explained, the government would take a cut in capital and declare the assets at Peenemünde to be worth 1,000,000–2,000,000 RM. This would enable the Siemans Company to acquire the station at less than 1 percent of its actual cost. It would also place the A-4 completely under the control of the Ministry of Munitions. Fortunately for the Army, this scheme was abandoned after it became apparent that its implementation would have interrupted progress on A-4 at a critical time in its development.

Later in the month, the Long Range Bombardment Commission was established within the Reichsministerium für Rüstung und Kriegsproduktion (RuK, or Ministry of Armaments and War Production). The first chairman of the commission was Professor Waldermar Petersen, formerly one of the directors of the Allgemeine Electrizitäts Gesellschaft (General Electric Company).

Another month passed and still the rocket program languished because of its lack of priority. Once again, Dornberger appealed to Speer, and once again his request was denied. This time (according to Dornberger) the reason given for the denial was that Hitler had dreamed that the A-4 would never reach England! In recent years the veracity of this story has been questioned. Speer does not mention it in his memoir *Inside the Third Reich*. Further, in correspondence with historian Mitchell R. Sharpe, he expressed doubt that Hitler would have delayed the A-4 for that reason.[1] Finally, the possibility that the dream never occurred is further strengthened by the fact that on 29 March (later in the same month the dream allegedly occurred), Hitler authorized the construction of a large bunker for firing missiles on the French coast near Watten. It seems possible that, knowing the Führer's skepticism for the project, Speer fabricated the story to quell further protests from Dornberger—a decision based on technical reasons could be argued against; one based on something as arbitrary as a dream could not.

Despite its low priority, the A-4 attracted the attention of Heinrich Himmler, head of the Schutzstaffel (SS). Himmler visited Peenemünde in early April 1943. In his conversations with Dornberger, the SS Reichsführer expressed the opinion that Hitler would soon change his mind regarding the A-4. He also offered to provide ''protection'' from sabotage and espionage for the project. Generaloberst (Colonel-General) Friedrich Fromm, Chief of Army Armaments who, along with General Emil Leeb accompanied Himmler on his tour, pointed out that Peenemünde was an army installation and the army alone was responsible for its internal security. Fromm tried to soften the abruptness of his refusal by adding that he would welcome having the SS tighten security on the remainder of Usedom Island and the adjacent mainland. Himmler agreed to do this and delegated the task to the police commissioner for nearby Stettin.

His initial thrust blunted, Himmler then tried a more direct approach in his efforts to become involved in the army's rocket program. As he left Peenemünde, he told Dornberger that he was very interested in the A-4 and that he could be of great assistance to the project. The Reichsführer promised to return to Peenemünde without Fromm and Leeb to continue his discussions with Dornberger. These were the opening moves in what became a battle over control of the A-4 between the Army and the SS.

Shortly after Himmler's visit, Dornberger became embroiled in another battle, the outcome of which would determine the continuation of the A-4 project. The Army was not the only branch of the Wehrmacht developing a long-range bombardment weapon. The Luftwaffe had its own project, the Fiesler 103 (Fi 103). The Fi 103 was a pulse-jet powered unmanned aircraft armed with a one-ton high-explosive warhead. It had the advantages of being relatively simple and inexpensive compared to the A-4. The Fi 103's engine consumed a low-grade fuel oil, while the A-4 required special propellants, some of which were difficult to transport and handle.

The Fi 103's disadvantages included its flight characteristics and the requirement for large, fixed launching ramps. The cruise missile flew at a constant speed (about 360 miles per hour), a constant altitude, and in a straight line. These characteristics made it vulnerable to both aerial interception and ground-based antiaircraft batteries. The A-4 struck at supersonic speeds, giving it the advantages of surprise and immunity to all known countermeasures. Further, the A-4 could be fired by mobile field units, which could launch a missile and move before being detected by Allied reconnaissance.

A committee of high-ranking persons including Speer, Luftwaffe Field Marshal Erhard Milch, Grand Admiral Karl Dönitz, and Colonel General Fromm, convened at Peene-

Wernher von Braun briefing a group of high-ranking Wehrmacht officers at Peenemünde, ca. 1943 (S.I. Negative #78-5935).

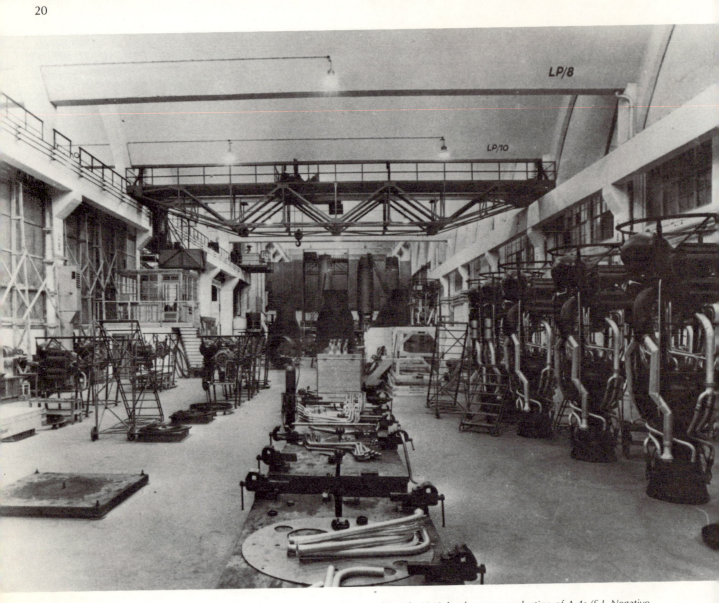

The pilot production plant at Peenemünde, one of three facilities designated in July 1943 for the mass production of A-4s (S.I. Negative #77-14248).

münde on 26 May 1943, to decide which weapon, the A-4 or the Fi 103, should be completed and deployed. The technical staffs responsible for each weapon presented briefings to the committee, which were followed by launches of two examples of each missile. Both Fi 103s crashed shortly after launch while the A-4s performed flawlessly and reached ranges of 160 miles. Fortunately for the Luftwaffe, the committee made its decision based on the technical briefings, not on the firing demonstrations. The decision was, since each weapon possessed certain unique advantages (and disadvantages), that the two would complement each other and should both be deployed.

Two days after the demonstration Speer called Dornberger (who had risen to the rank of Colonel) to inform him that he was being promoted to Generalmajor (Major General)[2] effective 1 June.

Dornberger and von Braun were summoned to Hitler's headquarters Wolfsschanze (Wolf's Lair), near Rastenburg in East Prussia, on 7 July 1943. When they took off from Peenemünde aboard a Heinkel 111 with Dr. Ernst Steinhoff, head of the Instruments, Guidance, and Measurements Department, at the controls, they carried with them models of the rocket, its proposed field handling equipment, the Watten bunker, and a film of the successful 3 October flight. Later that night, Hitler was shown the film while von Braun narrated. Dornberger continued the briefing and used the models to explain the tactical aspects of launching large missiles.

In contrast to the apathy shown by Hitler during his visit to Kummersdorf, this time he was enthralled as he watched the film of the A-4 ascending into the clear blue sky over Peenemünde. He asked Dornberger if it were possible to increase the size of the rocket's warhead to ten tons and if 2000 rockets could be produced per month. There were a few tense moments when the Führer's temper flared after Dornberger responded negatively to both questions. Overall, however, all went well for the Army's rocket builders. The A-4 was given the highest priority possible and Hitler apologized to Dornberger for having doubted the ultimate success of the project!

Three years after it was removed from the priority programs list, the A-4 once again enjoyed a high-priority status. With money and materiel again flowing into Peenemünde in large amounts, concrete planning for the missile's mass production, crew training, and tactical doctrine commenced.

1. Ordway, Frederick I., and Sharpe, Mitchell R., *The Rocket Team*, p. 43.
2. Generalmajor was the lowest German rank of General bestowed during the war. Because of this, individuals who held this rank have occasionally been referred to as ''Brigadier General'' in some American publications, this being the lowest American General Officer rank.

Mass Production

FOLLOWING HIS APPOINTMENT as the head of A-4 production in January 1943, Gerhard Degenkolb did little to ingratiate himself with Dornberger. Dornberger looked upon Degenkolb, a ruthless administrator previously in charge of locomotive production, as an outsider incapable of understanding devices as complex as the A-4. Further, Degenkolb was one of the individuals responsible for the reorganization of the German armaments industry in 1940. Prior to the reorganization, armaments production was supervised by the Armed Forces High Command and Ordnance departments of the different services. Afterward, supervision of the industry was transferred from the military to the civilian Ministry of Munitions. This was one of the events that led to the suicide of General Becker of the Ballistics and Munitions Branch of the Ordnance Department, a man Dornberger held in great esteem.[1]

In response to pressure from his superiors, Degenkolb was anxious to begin mass production of the A-4 immediately. Recent successful tests at Peenemünde had been mistakenly interpreted as a sign that the rocket was ready for production. Each rocket was still hand-crafted, however, and the missile's design still needed further refinement. Despite Dornberger's efforts to point this out, in July 1943 three facilities were ordered to prepare to begin production of the A-4. The proposed factories were at Peenemünde, the Zepplin Works in Friederichshafen, and at the Rax Works in Wiener-Neustadt. Degenkolb set a production goal of 900 rockets per month from the three factories. Karl Saur, chief of armament production and development in the RuK, insisted that 2000 missiles be produced each month. The official target figure was finally set at 1800 missiles per month and planning proceeded accordingly.

On the night of 17–18 August, the air raid sirens at Peenemünde sounded their alarms. This was not unusual—bombers often passed overhead as they entered German airspace from the Baltic. This time, however, the target was not Berlin or some other major city; the Royal Air Force (RAF) intended to disrupt the activities at Peenemünde.

For several years, intelligence reports hinted that "secret weapons" were being built there, but it was not until the spring of 1943 that A-4s and Fi 103s began to show up on aerial reconnaissance photographs. Analysts in England disagreed over the exact characteristics of the weapon. Sir Alwyn Crow, who worked on cordite solid-propellant

Because of Allied bombing, A-4 production was moved underground. The Mittlewerk plant, where nearly 6000 missiles were produced, was located beneath these hills in the Harz Mountains (S.I. Negative #79-13172).

rockets, postulated that the Germans were building a 100-ton solid-fuel rocket with an eight-ton warhead.

Professor Frederick Alexander Lindemann (Lord Cherwell) was unable to believe the Germans would squander their limited resources on a weapon as chimerical as the long-range rocket. He felt the Allies were victims of an elaborate hoax. Still others believed that liquid fuel rockets were being built at Peenemünde, but their estimates as to the missile's size varied greatly. Despite these disagreements, everyone (with the exception of Viscount Cherwell) did agree that some sort of significant work was taking place on Usedom Island and that the RAF should intervene.

One of the principal targets of the raid on Pennemünde was the settlement area where most of the key personnel lived. The pathfinder aircraft was slightly off-target, so the heaviest bombing occurred in the Trassenheide foreign prisoners camp. Overall, damage throughout the installation was heavy, but many critical facilities such as the supersonic wind tunnel, measurements laboratory, and liquid oxygen plant were unscathed. Dr. Thiel and Chief Engineer Walther were dead, along with 732 others. More than 550 of the casualties were from the foreign prisoners, who were locked in their barracks to prevent their escape during the raid.

Recovery from the raid was surprisingly swift; within six weeks, work resumed at the research station. Ruins of many demolished buildings were allowed to stand and subsequent construction was carefully camouflaged, giving the illusion that Peenemünde was abandoned. This ruse was successful for about nine months, during which time the facility worked unmolested.

The proposed A-4 assembly plants in Friederichshafen and Wiener-Neustadt were also bombed during August. These raids showed the vulnerability of surface installations to air attack, so Hitler decided to move A-4 production underground and directed Degenkolb to find a site for the plant.

In his search for a location for the underground missile factory, Degenkolb found a ready-made area in the Harz (pronounced ''Hartz'') Mountains next to the village of Niedersachswerfen near Nordhausen in central Germany. The site consisted of two parallel tunnels through a mountain with forty-seven cross galleries built in 1936 for use as an oil storage area. As early as 1941, consideration had been given to building an industrial complex beneath the anhydrite hills near Niedersachswerfen.

The establishment of the A-4 factory provided an opportunity for both the SS and the Ministry of Munitions to assume greater control over the missile program. A state-owned corporation, Mittelwerk, was formed to manufacture A-4s. With the advent of concentration camps, the Nazi regime found that by using prisoners it had a vast pool of cheap labor. This type of labor was supplied to many German industries, including Mittelwerk. ''Wages'' for the workers were paid to the SS, which operated the camps.

The first group of prisoners arrived at Niedersachswerfen in August. They were housed in tents in a work camp code-named ''Dora,'' which was a sub-camp of the infamous Buchenwald extermination camp. The following month saw the appointment of SS Brigadeführer Hans Kammler to oversee the construction of Mittelwerk. Kammler, who was originally trained as an architect and had once supervised construction

Layout of Mittelwerk. Each of the two main tunnels was over a mile long. Only half of the factory was devoted to A-4 (or V-2) production; the rest was used for V-1 Buzz Bomb and aircraft engine production (S.I. Negative #79-13170).

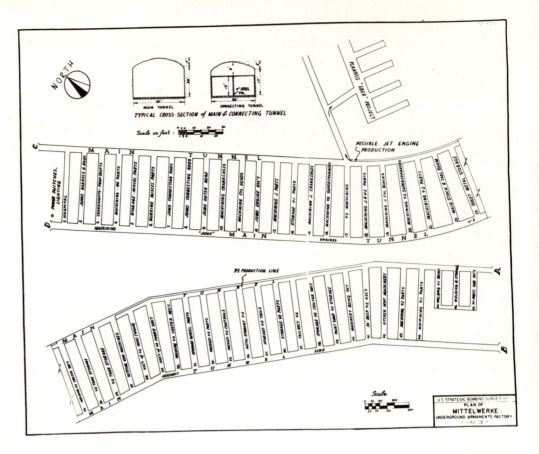

projects for the Luftwaffe, was already well known within the Nazi hierarchy for his involvement in the design and construction of the crematoria at Auschwitz and the destruction of the Warsaw Ghetto during the previous summer. Speer described him as "a cold, ruthless schemer, a fanatic in the pursuit of a goal, and as carefully calculating as he was unscrupulous."[2] Appointing Kammler to this position created a new layer of bureaucracy in the A-4 organization—a layer controlled by the SS.

Less than a month later, the prisoners' quarters were moved into the subterranean chambers beneath Kohnstein Mountain, where living conditions were unbelievably hellish. The prisoners were underfed and overworked. Most of the work needed to build Mittelwerk was done by hand. Prisoners choked on the anhydrous ammonia dust, which filled the air as they swung their pick-axes. Many died from exhaustion. Others died from the frequent beatings they received from the SS guards and prisoner-overseers, called "Kapos."

Those who didn't succumb to malnutrition, the 12-hour work shifts, or the beatings, usually died of disease. Sanitation was virtually nonexistent in the tunnels. Pneumonia, dysentery, tuberculosis, and typhus were rampant among the prisoners. "Medical care" for these diseases consisted of little more than light-duty, or bed rest in extreme cases. However, a prisoner had to have a temperature of 104° F before being admitted to the infirmary.[3]

Although Dora was not an extermination camp, most of the unfortunates detained there died; it has been estimated that 20,000 prisoners died there.[4] At first, the bodies were collected and shipped to Buchenwald for cremation. Later,

when Dora became an autonomous camp, a crematorium was built there. Political prisoners and common criminals made up most of Dora's population. The Kapos were most frequently selected from the ranks of the criminals. Because they were overseers, the Kapos were given special privileges such as above-ground billeting, private rooms, and extra rations. Rather than risk losing these few amenities, the Kapos would drive their fellow prisoners to work harder, often surpassing even the SS in their sadistic and brutal treatment of their comrades.

As the prisoners toiled in what has been described as the "Hell of all the concentration camps,"[5] the German government made the final plans needed to begin producing A-4s at Mittelwerk.

After a reexamination of the ability of German industry to provide liquid oxygen and alcohol to propel the rockets, the monthly quota was halved and a contract for a total of 12,000 missiles was awarded to Mittelwerk on 19 October. The total value of the contract was 480,000,000 RM with a unit price of 40,000 RM, subject to adjustment by Mittelwerk.

A branch of the RuK, the Rüstungskonter, selected a board of directors for Mittelwerk consisting of Dr. Ing. Kurt Kettler, SS Sturmbannführer Otto Forschner, and Otto Bersch. A fund of 10,000,000 RM was placed at their disposal to establish the factory. (This later proved insufficient, so a fund for an additional 50,000,000 RM was established by the German Trust Company for War Industries. The directors of Mittelwerk could draw from this fund at an interest rate of 3.25 percent.)

About a month after the contract was awarded to Mittelwerk, the board of directors submitted the delivery price for

On 19 October 1943, an order was placed with the state-owned corporation Mittelwerk for 12,000 A-4s at a unit price of 40,000 Reichsmarks (S.I. Negative #77 12528).

the A-4 to the RuK. The price for the missiles had risen considerably—the first thousand produced would cost 100,000 RM each, after which the unit price decreased in increments of 10,000 RM for every thousand A-4s produced until it reached 50,000 RM per missile.

The contract awarded to Mittelwerk also specified a delivery rate of 900 units per month. The initial layout of Mittelwerk was based on the earlier production target of 1800 missiles per month, so after the contract was awarded, space within the tunnels was reallocated. Cross tunnels 20—47 and the adjacent main tunnels were assigned to Mittelwerk for A-4 and Fi 103 production. The remaining space was used for manufacturing Junkers aircraft engines.

Orders for component parts were placed with German industry in late fall. To avoid bottlenecks caused by Allied bombing, the Speer Ministry directed that war production be dispersed throughout the Reich and that a minimum of two firms be contracted to supply each component. One notable exception to the latter policy was the construction of the steam turbine. The Ernst Heinkel Company in Jenbach, Tirol, was the only firm that could meet the specifications for that assembly.

On 10 December 1943 Albert Speer and his staff visited Mittelwerk. By this time, the factory was almost ready to start producing missiles. The facility was completely devoted to

mass production; gravity rollers, cranes, power conveyors, and rolling jigs were used to handle rockets and component parts. Each main tunnel was 5700 feet long, 35 feet wide, and 25 feet high. For a distance of about 800 feet from their entrances, the walls and ceilings of the main tunnels were faced in concrete. The rest of the walls and ceilings were painted white. This was reflective and improved lighting conditions and also helped waterproof the rock. The cross tunnels were, on the average, 30 feet wide and 22 feet high. Some were deeper when required for handling large A-4 components. Despite the modern features of the factory itself, the barbarity with which the prisoners were treated shocked the visitors so badly that some of them "had to be forcibly sent on vacations to restore their nerves."[6] Speer ordered construction of above-ground barracks to commence and directed his medical staff to take steps to improve the hygienic conditions in Dora.[7]

Entrance to one of the main tunnels of Mittelwerk (S.I. Negative #79-13171).

Entrance to the other main tunnels. Camouflage netting concealed the tunnel mouth. Pressure spheres for the V-1 are visible to the left of the entrance (S.I. Negative #79-13168).

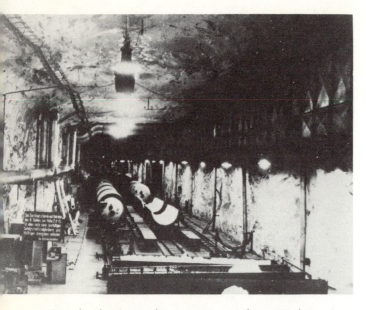

Several midsections under construction can be seen in this portion of the main tunnel (S.I. Negative #79-12324).

The cross tunnel where propulsion units were assembled (S.I. Negative #79-13166).

The first four missiles built by the Mittelwerk rolled off the assembly line on New Year's Eve, with mass production starting in January with an output of fifty rockets. During manufacture, the missile's midsection was assembled first. The sheet steel skin, after being cut and formed, was spot-welded to the internal longerons and ribs. A jig, similar to those used for aircraft fuselage construction, was used to align the pieces during assembly. Next, the midsection shells (which were assembled in halves) were placed in cradles where the electrical and pneumatic lines were installed, followed by a layer of glass wool insulation. The tanks were installed and the body shells assembled. The completed midsection assembly traveled along the main tunnel to cross tunnels #28 and 29 where the control compartment and propulsion unit, respectively, were assembled. After these sections were added, the vehicle continued along the assembly line to cross gallery #37 where the tail assembly was added. (Warheads for the rockets were not built at Mittelwerk and were attached to the missiles just before they were launched.) The completed rockets were finally taken to cross-tunnel #41, which had a 50-foot ceiling, for vertical tests. Upon completion of these tests, the rockets were lowered to a horizontal position and placed on rail cars for shipment. When production began at Mittelwerk, it took 15,000 man-hours to build each rocket. This figure was cut nearly in half (to 8000 man-hours) when the factory began operating at full capacity. Dr. Georg J. Rickhey became general manager of Mittelwerk in April 1944. In this capacity he was over the previously appointed board of directors and reported directly to Professor Karl Hetlage. Hetlage, head of the Rüstungskontor, bore sole responsibility for the Mittelwerk project in the financial and organizational planning section of the RuK. Kettler and Bersch remained to become directors on Rickhey's staff, while Forschner was transferred.

By mid-1944, over 8000 people were working on the A-4 assembly line, 5000 of whom were concentration camp prisoners. Fearing sabotage by the inmates, the Gestapo planted agents throughout Mittelwerk. German workers were not allowed to converse with the inmates except in the presence of an SS guard. The utilization of slave laborers to build the A-4 was eventually found to be inefficient, so they were replaced by skilled German labor. By the end of the war, only 2000 concentration camp inmates remained on the labor force at Mittelwerk.

During the first five months the factory was in operation, its monthly output climbed steadily. Then, production was slowed for two months until several problems with the missile's design (which were discovered during test firings in Poland) were corrected. Large scale production resumed in August 1944 (374 missiles) and continued until March 1945. From September 1944 through February 1945 more than 600 A-4s were produced at Mittelwerk each month.[8]

Mittelwerk was originally intended to be an assembly plant for contractor-built subassemblies. However, as the Russians advanced from the east and the Western Allies advanced from the west, many German factories were occupied. The Allied bombing offensive was also doing its share to erode Germany's arms manufacturing capacity. Because of this loss of industrial capacity, a plan was implemented to eliminate all subcontractors for A-4 components and completely fabricate the missiles at Mittelwerk. To accommodate the increased component fabrication, work was underway to build

Completed A-4 components, such as these tail units and body shells, were stored outdoors pending final assembly.

Table 1
Production of V-2 Missiles[a]

Month	Number	Unit Cost in RM
January (1944)	50	100,000
February	86	100,000
March	170	100,000
April	123	100,000
May	437	100,000
June	132	90,000[b]
July	76	90,000
August	374	90,000
September	629	80,000[c]
October	628	80,000
November	662	70,000[d]
December	613	60,000[e]
January (1945)	690	60,000
February	617	50,000[f]
March	540	50,000
Total for 15 months	5947	

[a]Taken from Armstrong *et al.* and Bilek and McPhilimy.
[b]Beginning 6/2/44.
[c]Beginning 9/23/44.   [e]Beginning 12/26/44.
[d]Beginning 11/8/44.   [f]Beginning 2/9/45.

Table 2
Disposition of V-2 Missiles[a]

Reaching England	1115
Reaching Continental targets[b]	1775
Airbursts	600–700
Total fired operationally	3600
In Mittelwerk at time of occupation	250
In field storage in English, American, and French occupied zones	1000
In storage in Soviet occupied zone	1100
Total accounted for	5950

[a]Taken from Armstrong *et al.* and Bilek and McPhilimy.
[b]In another source, The Report of the General Board, United States Forces, European Theater, *V-2 Rocket Attacks and Defense,* it is estimated that the number fired at targets on the European continent was 1950. This estimate is based on a study of ground incidents, captured documents and prisoner of war interrogations.

Before the A-4 was committed to operational use, crews practiced firing missiles in Poland. During these firings, field procedures and tactical doctrine were developed (S.I. Negative #77-4218).

Several rockets await launch during a training exercise in 1943 (S.I. Negative #A5367A).

second floors in some of the tunnels when the war ended.

Elements of the United States Army occupied Nordhausen and Mittelwerk in May 1945. Nordhausen was located in what had been designated as the Soviet Occupation Zone, so a hurried effort was made to evacuate as much materiel as possible before the Russians took possession of the facility. Prior to the Russian occupation, technical intelligence teams from both the United States and Great Britain toured Mittelwerk. One of the last to visit Niedersachswerfen was the Fedden Mission, headed by Sir Roy Fedden of Britain's Ministry of Aircraft Production.

The Mission arrived in Nordhausen on 19 June 1945. Their report of the trip includes descriptions of the idyllic local scenery and lovely weather. This information was included because Mittelwerk "made such a profound impression upon the members of the Mission."[9] Their impressions of the facility are best described by quoting directly from their official report:

> The Mission had been told that Nordhausen [sic.] was a large underground factory, and that they would see extraordinary production methods, but they had no idea that they would be brought face-to-face with such an undertaking. The reaction of the Mission to this visit . . . was one of the utmost revulsion and disgust. This factory is the epitome of megalomaniac production and robot efficiency and layout. Everything was ruthlessly executed with utter disregard for humanitarian considerations. The record of Nordhausen is a most unenviable one, and we were told that 250 of the slave workers perished every day, due to overwork and malnutrition. Some of the Mission visited a slave workers' encampment, talked to a Dutch doctor who had been there throughout the war, and saw many of the wretched inmates, who were in an apalling state, although receiving every medical attention now. They also saw stretchers heavily saturated in blood, a room in which there was a slab on which the bodies were drained of blood, and the incinerators in which the bodies were burnt. These are all facts which require to be seen to be fully appreciated. This terrible and devilish place has now passed into Russian hands and it is sincerely hoped that our allies will deal with it in a proper and adequate manner.[10]

1. Dornberger, Walter, *V-2*, p. 77.
2. Speer, Albert, *Inside the Third Reich*, p. 445.
3. Michel, Jean, *Dora*, p. 5.
4. *Prosecution Brief, Nordhausen War Crimes Trial*, National Archives Microfilm Publication M 1079.
5. Michel, *Op. cit.*, p. 5.
6. Speer, Albert, *Inside the Third Reich*, p. 441.
7. On 18 January 1944, Speer was admitted to the Hohenlychen hospital in Klessheim with what was diagnosed by Dr. Friedrich Koch of the University of Berlin as a pulmonary embolism. The Reichsminister remained hospitalized for more than two months, during which time these instructions were not carried out.
8. Due to the chaotic situation in Germany at the end of World War II and the subsequent lack of documentation, these figures, taken from Table 1, are estimates based on the recollection of Dr. Georg Rickhey, former general manager of Mittelwerk.
9. Fedden, Roy, *The Fedden Mission to Germany*, Combined Intelligence Objectives Sub-Committee, 1945, p. 75.
10. *Ibid.*, pp. 75–76.

Field Deployment Preparations

THE NEED FOR TRAINING PERSONNEL to prepare and launch the A-4 in combat was recognized early in the missile's development. In April 1942, a Training Command was established within the Versuchskommando Nord. This command was assigned the tasks of testing and evaluating the A-4 and its field handling equipment, developing tables of organization and equipment for future rocket batteries, and of training instructors for the proposed units. The training unit was headquartered in Karlshagen, just south of Peenemünde East.

The initial training course was divided into three phases. The first phase, known as A.I, lasted eight days and provided an introduction to the A-4. The second phase comprised two parallel seven-week courses: A.IIa for electronic training, and A.IIb for training in other technical aspects of the rocket. Following the second phase, the students were given written and oral tests. Based on the results, individuals were selected for further training in the shops and laboratories at Peenemünde or removed from the A-4 program.

Training was conducted in this manner until the A-4's priority rating was raised in mid-1943. Immediately following his meeting with Hitler on 7 July when the change in the program's status was ordered, Dornberger issued the orders needed to begin preparing the A-4 for deployment. In mid-July, the Lehr and Versuchs Batterie 444 (444th Training and Experimental Battery) was formed at Peenemünde. This unit was composed largely of military personnel from the VKN and was given the mission of developing the tactical doctrine for firing the A-4, training operational crews, and conducting final testing of the missile before its operational commitment. Oberst (Colonel) Gerhard Stegmaier commanded the 444th.

Within the staff at Peenemünde two schools of thought existed regarding the operational deployment of the A-4. One group, consisting mostly of engineers, scientists, and technicians, favored firing from a massive bunker that would contain storage, testing, and servicing facilities. The other group, mainly military personnel, felt the missiles should be launched by mobile field batteries. As a compromise, three batteries were planned. Two would be mobile while the third would fire from a fortified emplacement.

Remnants of the large firing bunker near Watten after it had been bombed by the Allies (S.I. Negative #80-15307).

Hitler authorized the construction of the large bunker near Watten, in the Bois d'Esperlecques in March 1943, and construction started several months later. The bunker was designed to contain storage facilities for 108 rockets, a three-day fuel supply, and a liquid oxygen plant. The entire project required 120,000 cubic meters (4,237,000 cubic feet) of concrete. Such a mammoth construction project could hardly be expected to go unnoticed by the Allies, who bombed the site in August. According to General Dornberger, the bunker "was left a fantastic heap of wet concrete, steel, and timber."[1] After the concrete hardened, the bunker was unsalvageable as a launch site, though work continued to try to save a portion of it to house a liquid oxygen plant.

Construction shifted to a nearby limestone quarry at Wizernes. The plan for the Wizernes site was even more grandiose than that for Watten. A 20-foot thick concrete dome was to be placed over the quarry. After the dome was completed the plan was to excavate the quarry from within and add supports for the roof.

About a month after the Lehr and Versuchs Batterie 444 was formed, Dornberger submitted a proposal for the organizational control of the A-4. Within this proposed organiza-

tion, Dornberger would command all A-4 field operations and would have a staff similar to other divisional artillery commanders. Dornberger further requested that he be relieved of his position as Chief of Wa. Prüf. (BuM) 11[2] and be appointed Long Range Weapons Special Commissioner of the Army (Beauftragter zur besonderen Verwendung des Heeres, abbreviated BzbV Heer).

His request was granted on 1 September 1943, when he was appointed both Artillery Commander 191 and BzbV Heer. The duties assigned to Dornberger as BzbV Heer were: (1) to accelerate the final development of the A-4 and its field equipment; (2) to establish a supply system for the procurement of all necessary raw materials and equipment; (3) to raise and train units to field the rocket; (4) to supervise production; (5) to conduct field trials of the A-4; and (6) to make all necessary preparations in France prior to the commitment of the A-4 to battle.

After establishing his headquarters at Schwedt on the Oder River, Dornberger organized his staff into a command group, an engineer group, and a supply group. These groups were concerned only with problems associated with the operational deployment of the A-4. Deputies were appointed to manage problems in areas such as logistics and operations.

The first operational unit, Artillerie Abteilung 836, was formed during October in Vierow, east of Lubmin. A month later Artillerie Abteilung 485 was formed in Naugard. Both units were motorized and each was approximately equivalent in numbers to a battalion. Each had three firing batteries, a headquarters battery, and a supply and service battery. There were three firing sections with one launch table apiece per firing battery, giving each Abteilung nine launchers.

Oberst Stegmaier was appointed Kommandant of the Long Range Rocket School in addition to his assignment as commander of the 444th. He also commanded the Artillerie Ersatz Abteilung 271 (271st Artillery Replacement Battalion), the reserve unit for the field batteries. Stegmaier established his headquarters, called Kommandostelle-S (Headquarters Stegmaier), in Köslin to supervise these numerous activities.

The quality of instruction at the Long Range Rocket School had improved tremendously since the previous year. Whereas the first groups of students in 1942 received lectures followed by periods of apprenticeship in the shops of Peenemünde, personnel of the 836th were taught using elaborate mockups, cutaway models, and hands-on exercises with actual equipment. The training program was expanded. In addition to the "A" course, which was attended by officers and others with engineering qualifications, another program, the "B" course was presented to those not scheduled to be placed in positions of authority. The B course lasted about six weeks and consisted of six sections. According to a former instructor assigned to the 3rd Battery of the 836th, who was captured by the Allies in November 1944, the phases of the B course were: B.I) propulsion section; B.II) steering mechanisms; B.III) thrust termination control; B.IV) power supplies and generators; B.V) Leitstrahl guide beam apparatus; and B.VI) fuels.[3]

Peenemünde had one major shortcoming as an artillery development center; because the rockets were launched over the Baltic Sea, it was impossible to determine their exact points of impact. Dye markers carried aboard the missiles marked the areas where they landed in the water, but more precise measurements were needed to prepare range tables and ballistic data for the rockets. Dornberger began a search for an overland firing range shortly after the 444th was formed.

This presented an opportunity for Himmler to become involved in the A-4 program. An SS training ground near Blizna, Poland, the Heidelager, was offered to the Army for use as a launch site. The impact area was in the Pripet Marshes nearly 200 miles to the northeast. The Army was somewhat hesitant to accept this offer mainly because of several unanswered questions regarding liability for damages caused by A-4 accidents. After being informed that the Reichsführer SS would be responsible for damages outside the Heidelager and that they need only concern themselves with safety in the immediate launch area, the Army accepted.

Barracks, vehicle shelters, and other facilities were built during September and October. A rail spur connected the Heidelager to the Cracow-Lemberg line. The launch area was enclosed with a double fence of barbed wire. The 444th moved to the Heidelager and began preparations for field trials of the new weapon. Firing began at the Heidelager on 5 November.

The temperature was a brisk 14° F. Lacking experience in launching the A-4 under field conditions, the firing personnel assumed that the frozen ground would support the portable launch platform. Unfortunately, this was not the case. During the preliminary stage, the rocket's exhaust impinged on the ground. The ground thawed and allowed one of the legs of the launch platform to sink. When the main stage order was given and the missile lifted off, it was already leaning noticeably. The rocket's guidance system was incapable of correcting the vehicle's path following its less than normal launch, and the A-4 crashed after only a few miles. This was the first of many problems that would be encountered during the firing trials in Poland.

Meanwhile, the Wehrmacht Operations Staff under General Alfred Jodl was deliberating over how best to deploy both the A-4 and Fi 103. They finally decided to field the long-range bombardment weapons under a single joint-services command. Hitler concurred and on 1 December 1943, signed the directive creating the LXV Armee Korps zbV.[4] The LXV Corps was a joint service organization, composed of personnel from both the Luftwaffe and Army. An army general, 62-year old Erich Heinemann, was selected as commander. His Chief of Staff was Luftwaffe Oberst Eugen Walter. The rest of the staff was divided between the two services. Heinemann, former Kommandant of the Artillery School, was considered to be uniquely qualified for the post because of his experience in developing tactical procedures for new artillery weapons. Field units assigned to the LXV Corps consisted of the 155th Flak Regiment for the Fi 103, and the A-4 units under the control of Artillery Commander 191. Corps headquarters was established in France at St. Germain. Dornberger moved his headquarters to Maison Lafitte but because of problems encountered by the 444th, he spent most of his time at Peenemünde or in Poland.

As both BzbV (Heer) and Artillery Commander 191, Dornberger was able to control both A-4 development and field deployment. He felt it was necessary to have both realms under a single authority if the A-4 were to reach operational status. This view was not shared by either the Wehrmacht Operations Staff or General Heinemann. Heinemann further believed that an officer with actual field experience should command the troop units, so he replaced Dornberger (despite the latter's protests) as Artillery Commander 191 on 29 December 1943. Dornberger's successor was Generalmajor Richard Metz, a veteran of the Russian front.

Dornberger still had plenty to do as BzbV (Heer)—several serious problems with the A-4 had surfaced at the Heidelager. During the early Heidelager firings, only 10–20 percent of the rockets successfully fired reached their targets. By the end of March, launchings had been attempted with 57 rockets. Only 26 of these left the ground, and only four impacted within the target area.

Three types of failures were observed. Some A-4s ceased firing less than 100 feet above the pad, some reached an altitude of 3000–6000 feet and exploded, while others traveled the full range, only to explode a few thousand feet above the target.

Despite these problems, training of the field units continued. Upon completion of the classroom phase of their instructions at Köslin, the units were relocated to the Heidelager to practice handling the A-4, observe a firing by the 444th, and finally conduct an actual firing themselves. In early 1944, the 3rd Battery of the 836th became the first field unit to fire at Heidelager. They were given seven rockets, three of which had live warheads. Of the seven, only four were successful. Rocket #1 failed to attain main stage (full thrust) and would not lift off. This rocket had to be returned for maintenance. Rocket #2 blew-up in the air. The third rocket was successful, and was reported to have landed 8 km from the target. As a reward for this, each member of the battery was awarded a bottle of brandy. The trim motors on the fifth rocket jammed, so this rocket had to be returned. Rockets 4, 6, and 7 were successfully fired, but the battery personnel were not informed as to the results of these launches.

It was against this backdrop of continuing problems and mishaps that Himmler struck on 15 March 1944—Wernher von Braun, Klaus Reidel, and Helmut Gröttrup were arrested by the Gestapo. Charged with sabotage, their crime had been to openly speculate about the possibilities of space travel at a party! Thus, it was deduced that they were not devoting their full energies to the A-4, thereby sabotaging the project. Dornberger immediately sought to have them released, submitting his protest through Army channels while Speer appealed directly to Hitler. Finally, after Dornberger stated that all three were indispensable to the project, they were released. Hitler assured Speer that von Braun was to be "protected from all prosecution as long as he is indispensable, difficult though the general consequences arising from the situation" were.[5] It appeared as though Dornberger had won—von Braun, Reidel, and Gröttrup were free—but Himmler had made his point. Nobody in the Peenemünde organization was beyond his grasp.

As problems continued at the Heidelager, it was theorized that the malfunctions were caused by acts of sabotage performed by the slave laborers in Mittelwerk. After being delivered to Peenemünde for test firing, the first four production missiles, bearing serial numbers 17,001–17,004, were found to have hundreds of defects. On 27 January 1944, the first of these to be flown, number 17,003, crashed and exploded after its engine faltered two seconds after liftoff.

To test the sabotage theory, the failure rate of rockets built at Peenemünde was compared to the Mittelwerk rounds. The failure rates were nearly identical, eliminating the possibility of sabotage. With this possibility eliminated, an intensive examination of the rocket's design was conducted. A faulty relay switch was causing the premature cutoffs. The cause of the explosions during ascent was a bit more subtle. This was traced to problems in the fuel-distribution pipes caused by vibrations during launch. Improvements in the connections on each end of the pipes, along with a redesign of the manner in which they were installed, corrected this problem. However, nearly 70 percent of the rockets fired still broke apart over the target. After further testing, glass wool insulation was placed in the spaces between the tanks and midsection body shell. This expedient helped and the success rate rose to 70 percent. Other minor modifications lowered the failure rate by another 10 percent. Finally, by the summer of 1944, through strengthening the forward portion of the midsection by adding a second layer of skin, the airburst problem was virtually eliminated.

Throughout the first half of 1944, while Dornberger wrestled with technical problems, General Metz worked to prepare the units under his command for deployment. Three months after assuming the duties of Artillery Commander 191, he inspected the batteries and was appalled at what he saw.

The 836th was found to be the best trained and equipped battalion, but still needed more practical training. The 485th was below strength in both men and equipment, and was just beginning organizational training. A third unit, Artillerie Abteilung 962, was not inspected because it was due to be disbanded and its personnel used to augment the other battalions. Overall, he was not satisfied with either of the battalion commanders, the readiness of the A-4 itself, the status of the special handling equipment needed, or the caliber of unit personnel. Metz concluded his report with a request for reassignment. This was denied by Heinemann, so he continued preparations for A-4 commitment.

A three-day exercise was held at the Heidelager on 18–20 May to assess the readiness of the A-4 weapon system. It was determined that another two or three months were needed before the missile could be deployed. The original tactical supply plan for the field batteries prescribed that rockets would be stored in field dumps throughout northern France. Many of these sites were nearly complete when the Allied D-Day invasion occurred on 6 June 1944. One of the effects of the invasion was the cessation of work on these sites. Throughout the summer, advancing Allied troops found these dumps.

A main supply dump was found at Hautmesnil, in a quarry next to the Caen-Falaise road. It consisted of a series of underground galleries through which a railroad spur had been extended from the main track. Other storage sites were found in the Normandy area at La Meauffe, Bois de Bougé, and Sottevast. Altogether, these sites provided the capacity for storing about 150 missiles in the area around Normandy. Numerous storage sites were also found in the Pas de Calais area. At Monchy-Cayeux, an above-ground dump was found. The facility contained 40 "rocket trolleys," a gantry with a five-ton winch, personnel quarters, and wooden shelters for the rockets. The storage capacity was estimated to be 28 rockets.

Prepared firing sites were also found in France, consisting of up to three concrete slabs camouflaged with a covering of dirt and grass. These sites were a direct result of the mishap that occurred during the first launch from the Heidelager. General Heinemann was present and saw the rocket go awry after the ground thawed beneath the launch table. He concluded that the A-4 could only be fired from prepared sites and ordered their construction shortly after becoming commander of the LXV Corps. Later tests at Heidelager showed such elaborate preparations were not needed; many successful firings were made from lumber-reinforced forest soil. Despite these later tests, Heinemann stood firm in his conviction that the A-4 could not be fired from anything but a prepared platform.

As late as the summer of 1944, plans were still being pursued to fire A-4s from the bunker at Wizernes. Allied bombing negated these plans just as at Watten the previous year. Six-ton "Tallboy" bombs were dropped on both sites in early July. The surviving portion of the Watten bunker collapsed after a direct hit on 6 July, while the area around the Wizernes dome was so badly churned up that further construction was impossible. On 18 July Hitler, despite his penchant for bunkers and monumental construction projects, ruled that plans for firing from large permanent sites need no longer be pursued. Thus, the decision favoring mobile field batteries over fixed emplacements was finally made.

July also saw the abandonment of the Heidelager because

of Russian advances through Poland. An area 10 miles east of Tuchel was selected for the new test site. Developmental firings continued from this location, which was code-named Heidekraut (Heather).

On 20 July 1944 an attempt was made on Hitler's life by a group of conspirators composed of high-ranking Wehrmacht officers. In the wake of this attempt, Himmler and his SS emerged even stronger than before. As the power of Himmler waxed, the power of the Army waned. During August, control over the A-4 was effectively wrested away from the Army. In two separate moves, first Peenemünde, then the A-4 field units were removed from Army control.

On 1 August, Peenemünde became the Electromechanische Werke, Karlshagen (Electromechanical Industries, Karlshagen) and Paul Storch, formerly of the Siemans Company, was appointed general manager of the new development plant. Along with this reorganization came the transfer of Dornberger out of the Peenemünde organization. The Electromechanisch Werke was charged only with operation of the developmental plant. Ownership of the facilities and equipment on Usedom Island remained vested with the government.

Himmler struck again on 8 August when he appointed Kammler as his Commissioner General for the A-4 Program. Throughout the firings in Poland, Kammler had been a regular visitor to the Heidelager. As he became more familiar with the missile, he also became more familiar with the personnel who were working on the A-4.

On 29 August, Hitler ordered that the A-4 offensive, code-named Operation Penguin, begin without delay. The next day, Kammler was placed in charge of the field commitment of the A-4. He established an improvised headquarters in Brussels and issued orders to the firing battalions to be ready to begin operations by 5 September. On 3 September, a total of 5306 personnel and 1592 vehicles were en route to establish firing positions between Antwerp and Malines. The large liquid-fuel rocket was about to become a weapon of war.

1. Dornberger, Walter, *V-2*, p. 176.
2. Wa. Prüf. (BuM) 11 was the abbreviation for the Heereswaffenamt Prüfwesen (Ballistik und Munition) 11, the Army's Ordnance Weapon Test Department 11 (under the aegis of the Ballistics and Munitions Branch of the Ordnance Department.) This organization was responsible for all Army rocket development at that time.
3. Felkin, S.D., *The A-4 Rocket—Further Information*, p. 3.
4. The letters zbV stood for "zur besonderen Verwendung," or, "for special employment."
5. Speer, Albert, *Inside the Third Reich*, p. 443.

V-2

An operational V-2 being prepared for firing (S.I. Negative #79-6558).

GERMANY UNLEASHED THE Fi 103 under the name "Vergeltungswaffe-1" (Vengeance Weapon-1), or more simply, V-1, on 13 June 1944. During the next several months, thousands of these cruise missiles were launched toward London. Throughout this bombardment the Nazi Propaganda Ministry touted the V-1 as a decisive weapon which was devastating England's capital city. These broadcasts also contained warnings of a new and even more terrible weapon, the V-2. It was promised that the V-2 would ultimately win the war for Germany. Hitler and the hierarchy of the Third Reich seem to have had high expectations for the A-4, which was to become the Vergeltungswaffe-2.

British intelligence had been receiving reports of German activity on the Baltic Coast since 1939, but it wasn't until mid-1944 that the Allies were able to obtain an example of the A-4 for examination. As luck would have it, two rockets were obtained within a month of each other. When the firing trials near Blizna began in 1943, the Polish Underground sent frequent reports to London regarding the new weapon being tested there. These reports continued through the winter and spring. Then, on 20 May, an A-4 landed in a swampy area near the Bug River. The rocket was nearly intact, and the Poles were able to hide it from the German search parties.

After the Germans gave up the search, the rocket was moved to a barn in the village of Hotowczyce-Kolonia. Working at a feverish pace, a technical team from the Research Committee of the underground Home Army dismantled and examined the rocket. During this examination, several preliminary reports were sent to London. On 12 July, the final report, which contained a 4000-word text, 80 photographs, 12 drawings, a map of the artillery range at Blizna, and three appendices with further information, was finished. This report, along with eight pieces from the rocket, was smuggled out of Poland aboard a C-47 Dakota and arrived in England on 28 July. The receipt of this cargo from Poland failed to attract the attention it deserved because components from another A-4 had been recovered only days before.

On 13 June 1944 an A-4 fired from Peenemünde strayed off course and impacted in Sweden. The Swedish government agreed to permit the British War Office to recover the wreckage. The missile broke apart in the air, so pieces were scattered over a con-

A V-1 Buzz Bomb shortly after launch (S.I. Negative #76-3443).

siderable area. Ultimately, however, over two tons of debris was collected and shipped to England.

Allied technical experts operating under the code name "Big Ben" then began the task of assembling the gigantic jig-saw puzzle. With wires and supports holding the torn and twisted pieces, the missile began to coalesce. Working around the clock, the Big Ben Committee unraveled the mysteries of this new weapon. By early September an amazingly accurate estimate of the rocket, its size, and its capabilities was made. Overall length was estimated to be about 46 feet, while the weight appeared to be about 14 tons. The odor of the fuel tank led to the conclusion that alcohol was the fuel. It was further deduced that liquid oxygen was the oxidizer and that both propellants were supplied to the combustion chamber by a turbopump. The range was estimated at between 185 and 200 miles.

The Big Ben Committee made only one major error in their judgment of the A-4: its method of control. The rocket recovered in Sweden had been used to test the radio-guidance system planned for the Wasserfall anti-aircraft missile. When this equipment was retrieved from the wreckage, it led the analysts to the erroneous conclusion that the A-4 was radio-controlled.

Despite this error, the Allies had an amazingly accurage concept of the A-4, so when the first missile hit London several days after the Big Ben Committee's report was finished, it came as no great surprise. The promised V-2 had finally arrived.

These V-2 pieces were recovered from a field in Belgium in November 1944. Using similar parts recovered in Sweden in June 1944, intelligence analysts were able to construct an accurate picture of the V-2 several weeks before its first use (S.I. Negative #80-3826).

The V-2 at War

U NDER KAMMLER'S IMPROVISED HEADQUARTERS, the V-2 field command was divided into two groups: Group North and Group South. Group North consisted of the 1st and 2nd Batteries of the 485th Abteilung and was ordered to occupy positions just north of The Hague. Group South, comprised the 2nd and 3rd Batteries of the 836th, was posted to the Laroche area while the 444th was sent to Fraiture, near Vielsalm in the Ardennes.

The distinction of opening the V-2 offensive went to the 444th, which fired two rockets toward Paris on 6 September 1944. Both failed. Two days later, after moving to a site 10 miles south of Houffalize, they achieved their first success. At 8:34 a.m., a rocket was launched which impacted near the Port d'Italie in Paris, 180 miles from the firing point. Later that night the first and second batteries of the 485th (Group North) fired two rockets from Wassenaar, a suburb of The Hague in Holland. Their target was about 1000 yards east of Waterloo Station in the center of London. The first landed at 6:43 p.m. at Chiswick. The second hit 16 seconds later near Epping. Three people were killed and ten injured in the first incident; there were no casualties caused by the second rocket. Firings continued from the Hague-Wassenaar area until 17 September, when the 485th withdrew to Burgsteinfurt because of Allied airborne landings near Arnhem. Meanwhile, the 444th moved to the island of Walcheren and began a special operation against London under the personal supervision of Kammler. Assisted by the 91st Technical Artillery Battalion, they launched six V-2s between 16 and 19 September. Finally, they had to withdraw to Zwolle because of the Allied assault on Arnhem.

Withdrawal of the 485th and 444th meant there were no V-2 units within range of London, so Kammler ordered the 444th to bombard Norwich and Ipswich from positions near Stavorem in Friesland. The 485th remained in Burgsteinfurt and commenced firing on Louvain, Tournai, Masstricht, and Liège. This continued until 30 September when the 2nd Battery of the 485th returned to The Hague and resumed operations against London. The 1st Battery continued to engage Continental targets. Further south, the 836th moved to the Euskirchen area and was launching missiles against Lille and Mions.

During the first weeks of the V-2 campaign, many problems were encountered due

A V-2 fell near the junction of Wanstead Park Road and Endsleigh Gardens, Ilford, England, in March 1945. Nine people were killed, eight houses demolished, sixteen houses so severely damaged they had to be demolished, and another one hundred forty-nine damaged (S.I. Negative #79-12323).

to a lack of staff control within Kammler's improvised head-quarters. Problems such as lost units, shipments of rockets arriving without warheads, lack of spare parts, and the ruin of alcohol tankers by using them to transport gasoline became all too frequent occurrences. To alleviate this situation, on 30 September the Oberkommando des Heeres, (OKH, the High Command of the Army) organized a divisional staff for Kammler. (It should be noted that this was done on Kammler's orders.) His division was called simply "Division zV," the zV meaning "zur Vergeltung" (for reprisal).

By this time, the 836th had moved across the Rhine to continue bombarding continental targets. On 4 October, Himmler ordered that firing on Paris cease. Eight days later Hitler ordered that all fire be concentrated on London and Antwerp, Belgium. Groups North and South were re-deployed to comply with the Führer's latest directive.

For those on the receiving end of the V-2, this new long-range bombardment weapon was most unpleasant. In London the V-1 had caused an average of 2.2 deaths per bomb. For the V-2, this more than doubled—5.3 deaths per round. Several factors contributed to the higher casualty rate. First of

all, the V-2 arrived without any warning. The relatively slow (several hundred miles per hour) V-1 was very noisy, and gave ample warning of its approach. Just before impact, the V-1's elevator would lock in the down position. This action was so violent that it disrupted the flow of fuel to the engine, causing it to become silent about 8–10 seconds before it hit. The sudden silence warned those in the area and allowed them several seconds to assume a protective posture; even lying down along a curb would frequently offer sufficient protection to survive a relatively close explosion.

Also contributing to the higher casualty rate was the intensity of damage caused by the missile. The average radius of damage within which houses were 75–100 percent destroyed was nearly identical for both the V-1 and V-2 (72 versus 76 feet). Within that radius, however, damage from the V-2 was more complete; that is, the rubble was more thoroughly pulverized, so those who weren't killed in the explosion were frequently buried and suffocated. The secondary zone of damage (50–75 percent destruction) was again virtually identical for both devices, but the radius for lesser damage was significantly greater for the V-2. In this zone of lesser damage many casualties were caused by glass splinters.

The final reason for the V-2's greater average lethality is the number of incidents where over a hundred casualties were caused by a single missile. One incident occurred in November at the New Cross Shopping Center. A V-2 struck just before noon, when the Woolworth's department store was crowded with Christmas shoppers. It took rescue workers nearly a week to remove 168 bodies from the ruins. There were also 108 persons seriously injured. Another midday incident, near the end of the V-2 campaign in March 1945, killed 115 and seriously injured 123. This occurred at Smith Market and Farrington, where a large number of women were lined up to buy groceries. Again, it took several days to exhume all the bodies from the rubble.

In all, an estimated 1115 rockets fell on England, about half of which (518) hit London and its suburbs. There were 2754 deaths and 6523 serious injuries in London alone from this barrage. In contrast, the 2344 V-1s which struck the city killed 5143 and seriously injured 14,756.

An even greater number of missiles struck targets on the continent, particularly Antwerp, Belgium. Following the single round that hit Paris on 8 September, no more rockets were fired against Continental targets until 13 September, when a single rocket struck near Brussels. The next day, which can be regarded as the real beginning of the rocket campaign in continental Europe, four more V-2s hit in the vicinity of Brussels. During the next month, Liège, Lille, Brussels, and Ghent were struck. Liège bore the brunt of the attack, with an average of over four incidents per day.

After Hitler's directive of 12 October, Antwerp, Belgium, became the focus of the continental V-2 campaign. Liège was important to the Allies as a rail and communications center and was located along the main supply route. Antwerp, however, was the main port for the delivery of supplies for the Allied forces in Europe. Hitler hoped to neutralize the port's effectiveness with the reprisal weapons. The center of the city and its docks were selected as targets for the missiles.

During October the 3rd Battery of the 485th completed its training at Heidekraut and joined Group North in the Burgsteinfurt area. A new battery, the SS Werfer Batterie 500 also joined Group North and was deployed around Hellendoorn-Zwolle in Holland. These units opened fire on Antwerp on 13 October. For the next two months an average of nine incidents per day were recorded in the Belgian capital. The tempo of firings intensified, reaching a peak of over 100 per week for three weeks beginning in mid-December. After the first of the year, the pace relaxed until the third week in February, when 91 incidents were recorded, only to taper off again and finally cease at 8:45 a.m. on 28 March 1945. An estimated 1950 V-2s were fired at continental targets, 1780 of those at Antwerp. The last London-bound V-2 had been fired several hours earlier, during the night.

By the time the 6½-month V-2 offensive ended, the units that fired the missiles had undergone several changes. On 1 January 1945, the 836th became the 901st Motorized Regiment and the 485th became the 902nd. Both were assigned to Kammler's Division zV. SS Werfer Batterie 500 became a battalion and was assigned to the 902nd. The 901st had three firing battalions; the 902nd had four.

The V-1 field command also underwent several changes during the latter part of 1944. The LXV corps became the XXX Armee Korps on 19 October 1944, and continued to have re-sponsibility for the V-1 until it too was disbanded. Kammler, always seeking ways to expand his sphere of influence, sought to control all V-weapons. He achieved this on 28 January 1945. The XXX Corps became the 5th Flak Division and, along with Division zV, became part of Armee Korps zV with Kammler in command. From the end of January through the end of March, the V-1 and V-2 were deployed under a unified command.

After the reorganization of the V-2 units, antiaircraft batteries, an engineer battalion, a supply battalion and three protective battalions were attached to Division zV for support. Each regiment, in addition to the missile batteries, contained a headquarters section, a workshop platoon for motor vehicle maintenance, two light antiaircraft batteries, a medical section, a supply section, an engineer battalion, and a maintenance company for motor fuel and oil transport. The V-2 Battery consisted of a Headquarters, Headquarters Troop, Launching Troop, Technical Troop, and Fuel and Rocket Troop. Within each battery there were many pieces of equipment—small arms, trucks, and communications gear—not unlike those found in any other military unit. Due to the unique nature of the V-2, however, there were also many items peculiar to these units.

The Technical Troop was in charge of unloading the missiles from the trains, and testing and preparing them for flight. There were specific platoons or sections assigned to each task.

The Fuel and Rocket Troop contained three platoons. The first platoon was responsible for transporting liquid oxygen from the rail site to the launching area while the second platoon handled alcohol and hydrogen peroxide for the propellant turbopump. The third platoon transported the rockets and warheads from the railhead to the technical troop. Sodium permanganate for the turbopump's steam generator was also handled by the third platoon.

There were three firing platoons in the Launching Troop, each with one launch pad. A launching platoon was expected to fire two or three rockets a day.

During the firing trials and early operational launches, it was found that the longer a missile was stored, the greater the chance that it would malfunction. Because of this, the missile storage depots were abandoned in favor of rapid rail transport from Mittelwerk directly to the field units. The missile trains, once loaded at Mittelwerk, were taken to a special outfitting station where the warheads, jet vanes, fuses, and containers of sodium permanganate were loaded. The trains then proceeded to the firing units. Each train carried 20 missiles. The trains were organized into three-car sections, each of which contained two rockets. Cars one and three held the missiles, while the middle car was used for the warheads, sodium permanganate, and graphite jet vanes. Camouflage covers over the cars concealed their cargo.

Regimental areas were selected by the Division Commander. The commanding officer of the regiment then assigned areas to his subordinate units. Launching points were selected based upon proximity to railroads, quality and type of roads, and concealment. Pine woods were preferred as the coniferous trees made aerial detection more difficult and acted as a wind screen for the upright rockets.

Upon arrival at the unloading point, the trains were met by the Railway Transport Officer, Regimental Quartermaster, Battery Quartermaster, and members of the Technical and

The Strabo crane ready for use (S.I. Negative #79-13217).

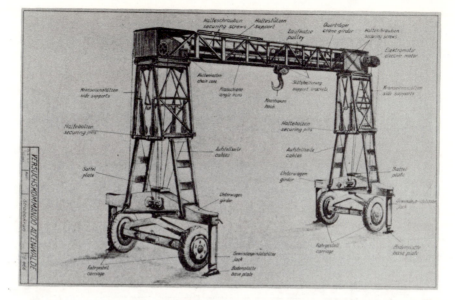

First version of the Vidalwagen, used to move rockets from the railway unloading station through the technical troop area. Later models had a pipe-frame fin protector and an aft towing attachment (S.I. Negative #79-13213).

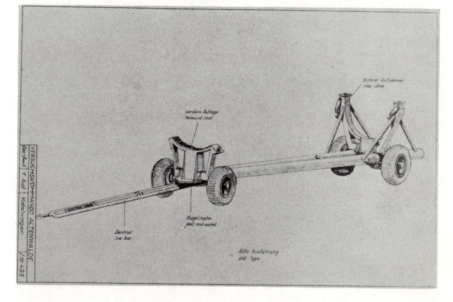

The Meilerwagen was used to transport the rocket from the technical troop to the firing troop (S.I. Negative #79-13193).

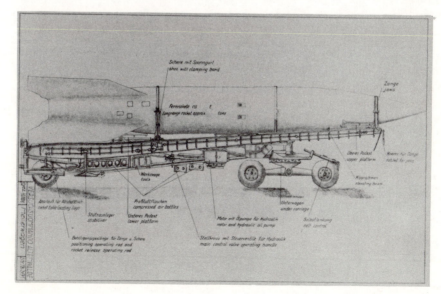

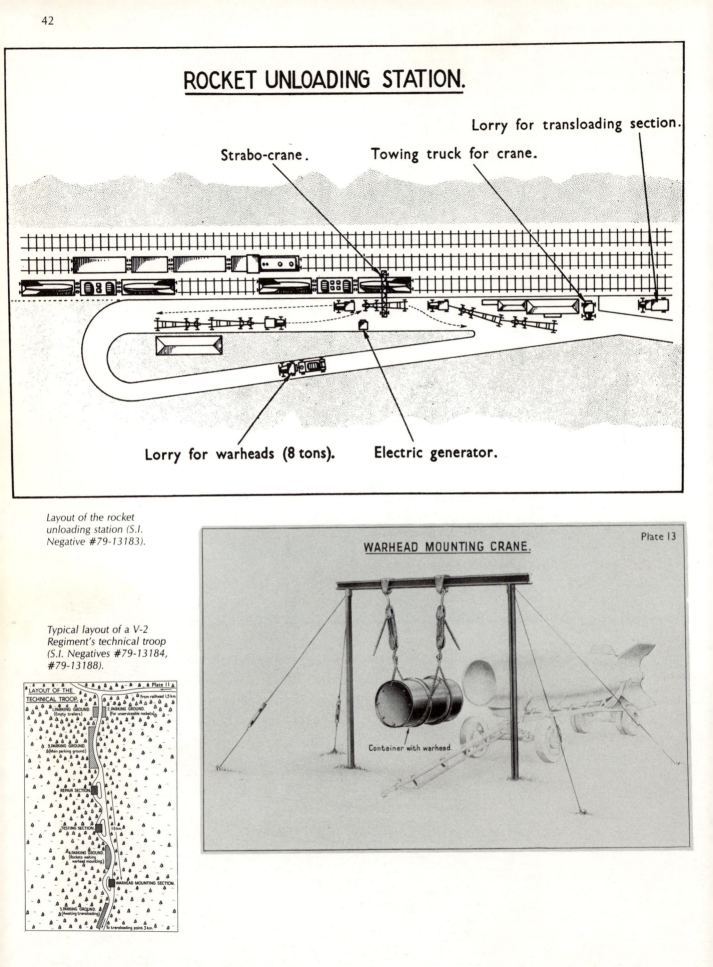

ROCKET UNLOADING STATION.

Strabo-crane.

Towing truck for crane.

Lorry for transloading section.

Lorry for warheads (8 tons).

Electric generator.

Layout of the rocket unloading station (S.I. Negative #79-13183).

Typical layout of a V-2 Regiment's technical troop (S.I. Negatives #79-13184, #79-13188).

WARHEAD MOUNTING CRANE.

Plate 13

Container with warhead.

Fuel and Rocket Troops. After the cargo was checked against the shipping voucher, the rockets were unloaded from the train using a portable crane called the strabo crane. The strabo crane consisted of a horizontal girder that rested on two scissor supports, which were raised by an electric motor. The crane could lift up to 16 tons. A block and tackle traversed the length of the horizontal beam to lift the horizontal rockets off the rail cars and place them on trailers called Vidalwagens.

The Vidalwagen was a lightweight trailer just over 46 feet long, used to transport a V-2 from the railroad to the Technical Troop area.

Technical Troops were located between their launching troop and the railway unloading station. As with the Launching Troop, type and quality of overhead concealment factored into site selection. Concealment for the Technical Troop was especially important because several large tents and parking grounds within the area were required. Additionally, it was desirable to locate the Technical Troop close to the Launching Troop so the rockets could be launched as soon after check-out as possible.

After arrival in the Technical Troop area, the Testing Section checked the missile. The checks included the propulsion unit, steering mechanism, alochol tank pressurization system, wiring, and the switch-over from ground to internal power. These tests usually took about three hours. If any faults in the missile's systems became apparent in the testing process it

was sent to the Repair and Tail Removal Section. This section performed only minor repairs, such as replacement of valves or servo motors. For major repairs, the rocket was removed to the field workshop (Feldspeicher), or sent back to the factory.

Upon completion of the test and any necessary repairs, the missile was taken to the Warhead Mounting Section. The warhead, still in its shipping container, was lifted into position with a block and tackle, and attached to the nose of the rocket. The exploder tube was filled and the nose and base fuses installed after the warhead was in place, and the shipping container removed.

Next, the rocket was moved to the transloading point where, using a strabo crane, it was transferred from the Vidalwagen to the Meilerwagen.

The Meilerwagen was used to transport the missile to the firing site and erect it on the launch pad. There were four main parts to the Meilerwagen: the chassis, lift frame, hydraulic lift, and camouflage cover. While in transit on the trailer the rocket traveled fins first.

The lift frame was attached to the chassis by a pair of trunnions. Two clamping collars on the frame supported and secured the rocket. One collar held the V-2 between the tail unit and mid-section. The other collar was smaller and encircled the rocket at the base of the warhead. Three (later reduced to two) movable platforms attached to the lift frame provided access to the rocket after it had been raised. Rungs welded to the right-side girder formed a ladder to reach the

At the launch site, the Meilerwagen was used to raise the rocket to a vertical position on the portable launch pad (S.I. Negative #76-2003).

platforms. Plumbing for filling the propellant tanks was also contained in the lift frame.

Two hydraulic cylinders elevated the lift frame. Oil for the hydraulic lift was stored in a cylindrical tank at the forward end of the chassis. A high-pressure oil pump powered the cylinders. The pump was driven by either a 14-horse-power gasoline engine or an electric motor.

A pipe framework and canvas camouflage cover were used to disguise the Meilerwagen. Sockets were provided on the trailer for attaching the frame.

The Launching Troop Rocket Supply and Accessories Column moved the rockets to the launch site. By the time the rocket arrived, the fire control vehicle, launch pad, and electrical cables were in position. The control vehicle was placed 100 meters from the launch pad behind the line of fire. Usually the vehicle was dug in to the depth of its tracks. Two-man slit trenches, 150–200 meters from the launch pad, were prepared for use by platoon personnel. If the overhead cover was insufficient, branches were sometimes suspended across the open areas over the firing platoon from overhead wires. The ground underneath the launch pad would have been reinforced, frequently with logs.

The Meilerwagen was brought within 50 feet of the launch pad, at which point the Firing Platoon Truck Section took charge of the missile. After the camouflage cover and rudder protection cases were removed, the control compartment batteries, alcohol filling connection, tools, and other accessories were placed in a box which was hung on a strut at the top (end) of the lift frame.

Hand winches were used to move the Meilerwagen up to the launch pad. Brackets on the pad engaged lugs on the trailer chassis to indicate that the two were properly aligned. After leveling the Meilerwagen by means of two extendable outriggers with end-jacks, the truck section began raising the rocket. When the lift frame was vertical, the rocket was suspended just above the launch pad. Any final adjustments to the position of the pad were made with levers and man-power.

The portable launch pad consisted of the launch table, blast deflector, cable mast, valve box, five-way coupling, and oxygen tank topping-off connection. The rocket stood on the launch table, which was supported by four tubular legs. Underneath the table was the blast deflector. It was made of heavy steel plate in the shape of a four-sided concave pyramid. A mast attached to the table carried an electric cable to the missile's control compartment. The cable provided power to the rocket until launch, when it was cast off.

During testing, fueling, and launching, the valve box was used to regulate the supply of air pressure to the missile. Electrical connections for the rocket were also contained in the valve box. The terminals for the igniter were located on the exterior of the box, on the left side. When traveling, the box was removed from the launch table and carried in another vehicle to prevent damage. It attached to the table by two brackets. The five-way coupling was an adjustable coupling extending from the valve box to the connection near the base of the rocket between fins II and III. An individual launch pad could be used for 30–40 launches.

The launch table supporting plates were raised until they just touched the rocket's fins. Next, the clamping collars were lowered using a ratchet until the rocket rested on the launch pad. After the clamping collars were released, the Meilerwagen was withdrawn 90 cm from the rocket, which was traversed 90° on its turn-table so the fueling connections faced the working platforms. The platforms were lowered, the cable mast raised, and the valve box and the five-way coupling attached to the launch pad.

Two collimeters, 90° apart and about 90 yards from the launch pad, were used to ensure that the rocket was vertical. Necessary corrections were made using jacks in the launching table.

The next step was to prepare the rocket for another series of preflight tests. Three jet vanes were installed; the fourth was left off until after a visual inspection of the combustion chamber interior. A wooden platform placed on the blast deflector permitted access to the chamber. Upon completion of the inspection, which was to make sure that the propellant injection nozzles were clear of dirt and grease, the platform was removed and the fourth jet vane installed.

Meanwhile, the batteries were installed in the control compartment and the pressure cylinders in the compartment charged. The five-way coupling was connected to the valve box and the rocket.

Tests were made of the steering mechanisms and controls, rocket motor, switch over from ground to internal power, and the rocket's internal sequencing mechanisms. These tests were controlled from the fire control vehicle (Feuerleitpanzer). The fire control vehicle was a half-track vehicle, the aft portion of which was armored. Within the vehicle there were panels for steering tests of the V-2, rocket motor tests and launch control. Seats and observation slits with two-inch thick windows were provided for the panel operators and the firing officer. There was a communications compartment equipped with a telephone and either a 10- or 20-line switchboard. Through the switchboard, communications could be maintained with Launch-Troop Headquarters, the other two launching platoons, and the launch site.

A three-section extendable ladder, the Magirus ladder, was used when the rocket was on the launch pad to reach those parts inaccessible from the Meilerwagen work platforms. The ladder was mounted on a two-wheeled carriage and could be moved short distances within the launch area. For movement over longer distances, it had to be carried in a truck. Fully extended, the ladder had a length of 56 feet. The ladder's elevation could be adjusted to any angle.

The V-2 consumed four propellants: liquid oxygen (A-Stoff), alcohol (B-Stoff), hydrogen peroxide (T-Stoff), and sodium permanganate (Z-Stoff). Alcohol and oxygen were the main propellants, while the hydrogen peroxide and sodium permanganate were used to generate high-temperature steam to power the missile's turbopump. Each propellant had its own transport vehicle.

When the rocket motor and steering tests began, the alcohol, liquid oxygen, and hydrogen peroxide tankers were brought into position. During testing, preparations were made for fueling. Also during the tests, the seven pressure cylinders in the propulsion unit were charged.

Propellant transport and loading were the responsibility of the Fuel and Rocket Troop. The Fuel and Rocket Troop unit area consisted of parking grounds and billets. These units were arranged for accessibility to the railway unloading stations and main supply routes in such a way as to preclude congestion in the area as liquid oxygen, alcohol, hydrogen peroxide, and rockets were delivered. The preferred arrangement was for each battalion to have separate unloading sta-

After the warhead was attached, the missile was transferred from the Vidalwagen to the Meilerwagen (S.I. Negative #76-2755).

A ratchet system was used to lower the rocket from the Meilerwagen lift frame onto the launch pad. After the rocket was in place on the launch pad, the Meilerwagen lift arm was retracted slightly and preparations were made for fueling the missile (S.I. Negatives #76-2002, #79-13186, #79-13189, #79-13185).

46

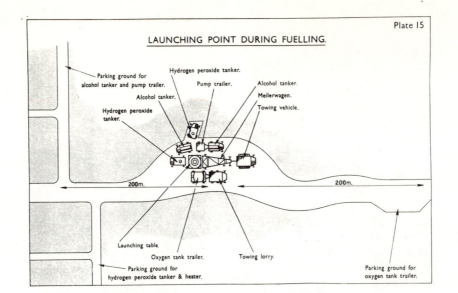

LAUNCHING POINT DURING FUELLING.

Parking ground for alcohol tanker and pump trailer.
Hydrogen peroxide tanker.
Pump trailer.
Alcohol tanker.
Alcohol tanker.
Meilerwagen.
Towing vehicle.
Hydrogen peroxide tanker.

200m.   200m.

Launching table.
Oxygen tank trailer.
Towing lorry.
Parking ground for hydrogen peroxide tanker & heater.
Parking ground for oxygen tank trailer.

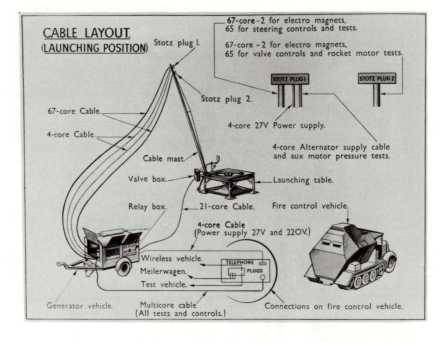

CABLE LAYOUT. (LAUNCHING POSITION)

67-core-2 for electro magnets, 65 for steering controls and tests.
67-core-2 for electro magnets, 65 for valve controls and rocket motor tests.

Stotz plug I.
Stotz plug 2.

STOTZ PLUG I   STOTZ PLUG 2

67-core Cable.
4-core Cable.

4-core 27V Power supply.

4-core Alternator supply cable and aux motor pressure tests.

Cable mast.
Valve box.
Launching table.

Relay box.
21-core Cable.
Fire control vehicle.

4-core Cable (Power supply 27V and 220V.)

TELEPHONE PLUGS

Wireless vehicle.
Meilerwagen.
Test vehicle.

Generator vehicle.
Multicore cable (All tests and controls.)
Connections on fire control vehicle.

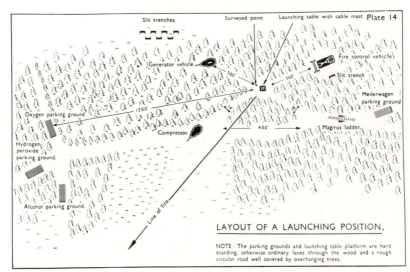

Plate 14

Slit trenches.   Surveyed point.   Launching table with cable mast.

Generator vehicle.
Fire control vehicle.
Slit trench.
Oxygen parking ground.
Meilerwagen parking ground.
1200'
Compressor.
Magirus ladder.
Hydrogen peroxide parking ground.
400'
Alcohol parking ground.
Line of fire.

LAYOUT OF A LAUNCHING POSITION.

NOTE: The parking grounds and launching table platform are hard standing, otherwise ordinary lanes through the wood and a rough circular road well covered by overhanging trees.

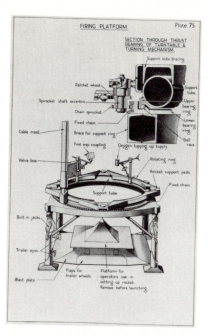

The portable launch pad (S.I. Negative #79-13182).

The fire control vehicle (Feuerleitpanzer) (S.I. Negative #79-13210).

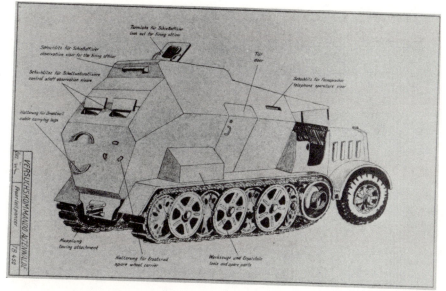

Inside the fire control vehicle, consoles were provided for tests of the propulsion unit, steering mechanisms, and thrust termination devices in addition to launch control (S.I. Negative #79-13215).

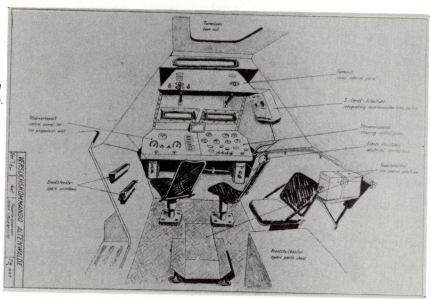

The fire control vehicle communications compartment (S.I. Negative #79-13199).

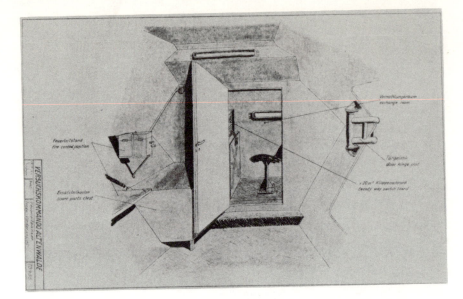

Rocket motor panel from the fire control vehicle (S.I. Negative #79-14836).

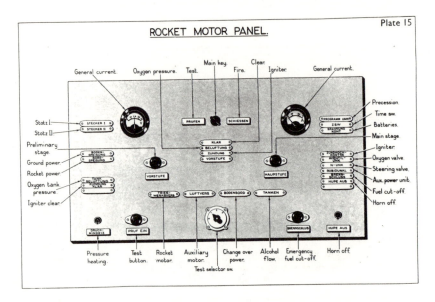

Rocket steering mechanism test panel from the fire control vehicle (S.I. Negative #79-14835).

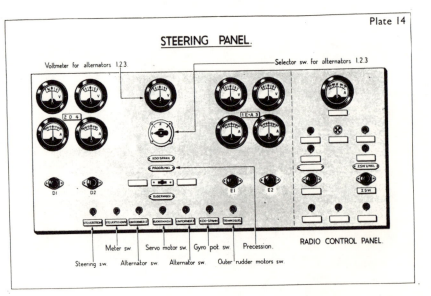

Liquid oxygen was transported to the launch site in a trailer that held enough for one rocket (S.I. Negative #79-13214).

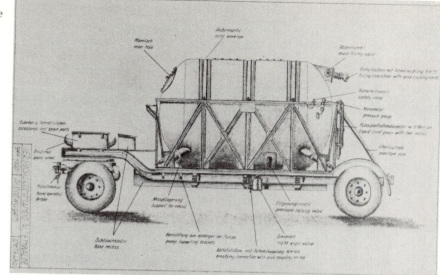

Two alcohol tankers were needed to fuel one rocket (S.I. Negative #79-13208).

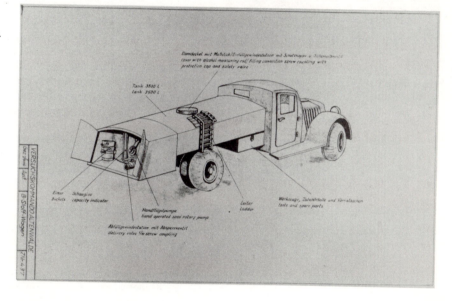

Ready for launch (S.I. Negative #79-1634).

tions for each major supply item, but this was not always possible. The emphasis in the deployment of the Fuel and Rocket Troop was to disperse the required vehicles in parking areas along the main supply route.

Alcohol was delivered to the launch site by a tank truck that held 2900 liters (765 gallons) of rocket fuel. An elliptical tank was mounted on a 3-ton truck chassis. Two tankers were required to launch one rocket. The alcohol pump was mounted on a two-wheel trailer. A 300 cc single-cylinder engine powered the rotary pump. The pump could fuel the rocket from both alcohol tankers simultaneously.

After the rocket was fueled, the oxygen tank was filled. Liquid oxygen was pumped by a portable pump unit fitted in a lifting-frame. The same pump was used to fill the transport trailer at the railhead. It normally took 20 minutes to fill the oxygen tank.

A four-wheel trailer with a cylindrical tank was used for the liquid oxygen. It held 6750 kilograms of oxygen, which, allowing for evaporation, was enough for one rocket. The tank assembly was made from an inner aluminum alloy tank and an outer body. Glass wool was used as an insulation between the inner tank and outer body. An eight-ton tractor was used to haul the liquid oxygen trailer.

Five minutes after they began to fill the liquid oxygen tank, the Fuel and Rocket Troop began to fill the hydrogen peroxide measuring tank on the Meilerwagen, which held 126 liters. Hydrogen peroxide was carried in a tank truck similar to the one used for the alcohol. The tank on this truck, however, was slightly smaller, with a 2120 liter (560-gallon) capacity. This was enough peroxide for 16 rockets. The pump for the peroxide was built into the back of the road tanker. When the measuring tank was full, the connections between it and the road tanker were closed. Hydrogen peroxide is extremely corrosive, so all pump lines were flushed with water after use. The T-Stoff tank in the rocket's propulsion section was filled from the Meilerwagen tank. Finally, the sodium permanganate, which was transported in its own container, was poured into the Z-Stoff tank.

The warhead fuses were armed, all access hatches closed, and final preparations for launching the rocket made. The Meilerwagen lift frame was lowered and the trailer removed from the area. If the rocket was equipped with an integrating accelerometer this had been set for the desired cut-off velocity during testing. For radio-control cutoff the ground equipment, called Campania, was placed 6–12 km behind the rocket, in line with the firing direction.

If a fully fueled rocket was allowed to stand very long before being launched, problems were often encountered with components freezing due to the liquid oxygen. To prevent these problems, two additional items of special equipment were provided: a heater for the hydrogen peroxide and a hot air blower. The hydrogen peroxide heater was intended for use when the outside temperature was below 20°C Before being loaded into the rocket, the peroxide was warmed to 40°C. The heater consisted of a double jacketed chamber with an alcohol jet. Water between the inner and outer chambers was heated by the flame. This heater was seldom used, even in winter, for none of the personnel involved liked the idea of using an open flame in close proximity to the hydrogen peroxide.

The hot air blower provided a jet of hot air into the tail section of the rocket to prevent the servo motors and valves from freezing. The blower was powered by a two-horsepower, two-stroke engine. It was not used in hot weather or if the rocket could be fired within one hour of fueling.

The rocket was traversed so that fin III faced the line of fire, the igniter installed, and the final steering tests made. During the final tests, the gyroscopes were switched on. All vehicles and personnel were evacuated from the launch site. When all was ready and he was satisfied there were no enemy aircraft in the area, the battery commander issued the launching order to the firing platoon, and the rocket was fired.

In March 1945, the first tactical use of large missiles occurred. On 17 March, the 500th SS Battalion fired eleven missiles at the Ludendorf Bridge in Remagen, Germany. One of the missiles hit German-held territory seven miles east of Cologne, 40 miles short of the target. The remaining rounds averaged a deviation of 1.1 miles in range and 2.5 miles in line. This is good when one considers that the range was 130 miles and that the target computations were hurriedly done in the field.

However, one must weigh the effectiveness of this attack and the strategic launches of the V-2 against the effort required to mount the campaign. The V-2 caused severe damage. In addition to the previously mentioned casualties and damage in London, in Continental Europe 5400 persons were killed, 22,000 wounded, and 90,000 houses were destroyed by the missiles. Because of these attacks, manpower had to be diverted from otherwise necessary military functions to civil defense. In order to keep the civilian work force from leaving the area, the passive air defense systems in Antwerp and Liège had to be overhauled.

From the German perspective, the offensive was extremely expensive, tying up considerable quantities of men and equipment. Each firing battery, which could launch up to nine missiles per day, contained 152 self-propelled vehicles, 70 trailers and five bicycles. The strength of each battery was over 500 men. Nine missiles could deliver $7\frac{1}{2}$ tons of high explosives—less than the maximum load of single B-17 Flying Fortress.

And, after all, England was not terrorized into surrender as Hitler hoped, and the effect on the flow of supplies through Antwerp and Liège was negligible, leading one to the conclusion that the V-2 failed as a weapon of war.

Despite their failure as weapons, the use of V-2s was far from over. In the years ahead, V-2s would continue to fly—not over the English Channel, but over the steppes of Russia and deserts of the southwestern United States.

Reaping the Harvest

THE UNITED STATES ARMY RECOGNIZED the gap in rocket development between the United States and Germany, and initiated Project Hermes on 15 November 1944 for research and development of ballistic missiles. The General Electric Company was contracted to conduct the project for the Army's Ordnance Corps. During December, it was decided to study the V-2 as a part of Hermes. Several months later, in March 1945, the War Department initiated Project Paperclip, the program to recruit German scientists and engineers to work under contract in the United States.

Meanwhile, elements of the advancing Allied armies found V-2 launch sites and equipment. One such instance occurred near Hellendoorn, Holland. Canadian forces sweeping through the area found a launch site previously used by the 500th SS Battalion in a wooded area on the outskirts of town. Local residents estimated that, prior to 20 March, about 160 rockets were fired from there at a rate of five per day. Craters in the area revealed that some rockets crashed shortly after liftoff.

British units advancing through Hannenberg, Germany (near Leese) discovered an outdoor missile dump. According to Dr. Georg Rickhey, General Manager of Mittelwerk, over 2000 V-2s were in storage throughout Germany when the last operational firing took place on 28 March 1945.

Half of the missiles in storage were in the Soviet occupation zone, 515 of which were developmental models consigned to salvage. Another thousand rockets were scattered throughout the British, American, and French occupation zones. Most of the missiles were missing some or all of the control compartment components necessary to guide them as they flew. Each of the victorious Allied countries was anxious to acquire rocket hardware, particularly the United States and Great Britain. The competition to recover V-2 materiel became so intense that on 4 May, orders were issued to Allied units freezing all missile hardware in Europe until the question of allocating the technological treasure trove was resolved. Great Britain sought to secure at least 150 missiles. Thirty were for their Army's V-2 flight research program, Operation Backfire; the rest were for evaluation of the Air Ministry. The United States wanted missiles to fire for the Hermes Project.

Elements of the United States Army occupied Mittelwerk in April and found about

This missile was one of several captured by British units operating near Leese, Germany (S.I. Negative #79-12330).

Canadian soldiers were shown the log platforms which were used to support V-2 launch pads used by the 500th SS Werfer Abteilung outside Helendoorn, Holland (S.I. Negative #79-12331).

An American soldier inspects a V-2 on a rail car captured at Bromskirchen, Germany (S.I. Negative #79-1639).

Underneath Kohnstein Mountain, about 250 missiles were found in various stages of completion on the Mittelwerk assembly line (S.I. Negative #75-15871).

250 rockets in various stages of completion on the assembly line. As Nordhausen was in the area scheduled to be placed under Russian control, there was a hurried effort to evacuate as much materiel from the underground factory as possible. Ultimately, 640 tons of equipment requiring over 300 railroad cars to move, were shipped from Nordhausen. This equipment was taken to Antwerp for shipment to the United States. Included in the components loaded on the Liberty Ships bound for America were six V-2 tail units requested for Operation Backfire. These were unloaded and turned over to the British before the ships set sail.

The Russians captured Peenemünde in March 1945. By the time they arrived, however, the facility was a ghost town. Fearing capture by the Red Army, the rocketeers had long since left. They first moved to Bleicherode, near Nordhausen, then finally migrated farther south, to a mountainous area near the German-Austrian border.

When the rocketeers left Peenemünde, they took their technical records with them. Within these records were the results of nearly 15 years of experimental work. The value of these documents cannot be calculated—whoever inherited them could continue the work started by the Germans. Von Braun realized the value of the files and detailed Dieter Huzel and Bernhard Tessmann to hide them.

They selected an unused mine near Goslar, north of Nordhausen. The location was supposed to be a secret known only by Huzel and Tessman, so the soldiers who helped them move the documents stayed in the backs of the trucks as they traveled to the site. As far as the owner of the mine was concerned, he was told only that these were classified documents. After the files were stored in what was once a powder magazine, the gallery leading to the room was sealed using dyanamite.

Their job accomplished, Huzel and Tessmann split up. Tessmann returned to Bleicherode; Huzel remained in Goslar to check the results of the blasting job in the mine one more

time. He remained there for two days, visited an old friend nearby, then hurriedly left when he heard that American troops were approaching.

Huzel arrived in Bleicherode to find the rocketeers had begun their flight south. He detoured to Berlin to fetch his fiancee and move her out of the path of the rapacious Russian Army, then also fled south. Finally, several days later, he rejoined his comrades in Oberammergau, a town near the Austrian border.

Huzel found that another, more sinister group of people were in Oberammergau: the SS. Apparently Kammler had posted guards on the missile development team. Fearing the SS, the group opted to migrate once more, to the Haus Ingeborg in Oberjoch near the Adolf Hitler Pass.

On 15 April 1945, Huzel and Tessmann sought Wernher von Braun and his brother Magnus to brief them on the disposition of the technical files. The next two weeks were spent exchanging stories and playing chess. The group discussed their future and their options. They finally decided to take their chances surrendering to the Americans. Magnus von Braun was dispatched on a bicycle to contact the American forces in Reutte, Austria. On 2 May 1945, they surrendered to elements of the 44th Division.

Kammler was not captured. In fact, the Peenemünde group hadn't seen him for some time. Dornberger, in his memoir, *V-2*, describes how his last contact with Kammler was early in April when the evacuation from Oberammergau was ordered. In the last months of the war, Kammler refused to quit. With fanatic zeal, he drove himself and those under him, always believing that the war could still be won. He was directed to command the final defense of Czechoslovakia, and he apparently died there. The circumstances of his death have never been clear, and it appears likely his adjutant shot him to prevent his capture.

Several days after their surrender, the Germans were taken to Garmisch-Partenkirchen for interrogation and processing. Eventually, over 400 people were assembled there. During the interrogations, the location of the hidden documents was revealed and these were recovered and sent back to the United States.

Although the Russians did not capture the top rocket specialists or the technical files, they did get Peenemünde itself and Mittelwerk after it was turned over by the Americans.

Quite a lot of materiel had been evacuated by the Americans, but it was almost exclusively restricted to rocket parts; the production machinery was still there. The factory was stripped clean by the Soviets, who then began building and launching V-2s in the steppes of central Asia. They continued launching V-2s and V-2-derivatives for several years after the war.

Meanwhile, the British round-up of V-2 hardware continued. Early in May 1945, it was proposed that German personnel fire captured V-2s for study and evaluation. The British 21st Army group was asked by the Supreme Headquarters, Allied Expeditionary Force to place a brigade headquarters under their direct control for execution of the project, which was code-named "Backfire." The headquarters selected was the 307th Infantry Brigade, commanded by Brigadier L.K. Lockhart. Upon dissolution of the Supreme Headquarters Allied Expeditionary Force on 14 July, the headquarters responsible for Backfire became the Special Projectile Operations Group (SPOG).

In May 1945, many engineers and scientists who had worked at Peenemünde surrendered to American forces operating near Reutte, Austria. Shown here are (left to right) Charles L. Stewart, U.S. Counterintelligence Corps; Lt. Col. Herbert Arter, a member of General Dornberger's staff; Dieter K. Huzel; Wernher von Braun (whose arm is in a cast after a car accident several months earlier); Magnus von Braun; and Hans Lindberg (S.I. Negative #77-11215).

British-collected V-2 materiel was shipped to the Krupp Naval Gun proving ground near Cuxhaven, Germany. German prisoners of war and civilian specialists assembled and launched three rockets in a British-supervised technical evaluation code-named "Operation Backfire" (Photo courtesy of Mitchell R. Sharpe, S.I. Negative #76-15729).

When Backfire was first conceived, it was expected that many complete, ready-to-launch rockets would be captured. This was not the case. All of the captured rockets were incomplete; most were missing critical control-compartment components. By mid-August the program had assumed two phases: (1) the assembly and production of rockets; and (2) the actual firings. Throughout the summer and early fall of 1945, SPOG expended 200,000 man-hours with a work force of over 200 persons in the search for V-2 parts.

Since the Backfire launchings were to be duplicates of war-time firings, field equipment also had to be collected. This frequently proved to be as difficult as finding critical rocket parts. All of the field equipment had been left out-of-doors for the past few months without any maintenance. Most pieces had been vandalized by retreating Germans, souvenir-hungry Allied soldiers, or local civilians. The process of recovery and refurbishment of Meilerwagens, Vidalwagens, launch pads, and other required equipment became nearly as complex as the preparation of the rockets themselves.

The captured materiel was assembled at the Krupp Naval Gun Testing Ground at Altenwalde near Cuxhaven, on the North Sea. It had originally been planned to launch about 30 missiles so all methods of fuel cutoff control and flight guidance could be examined. Due to shortages of critical components, only eight rockets could be assembled. Of these, only three were scheduled for launch. These rockets were equipped with time switches to control fuel cutoff.

German prisoners of war prepared and fired the rockets. They were divided into two groups. The first consisted of soldiers and civilians who assembled and launched the missiles. It was a military-style unit, called AVKO for Altenwalde Versuch Kommando, under former V-2 Regiment Commander Lieutenant Colonel Weber. The other group was made up of civilian experts detained for interrogation in Brockeswalde. In an effort to check the accuracy of information acquired from either group, the two were segregated. General Dornberger was also present at Cuxhaven for a few weeks, but was kept away from both units.

Finally, he was sent to England and tried as a war criminal.

His crime had been to launch V-2s against the open city of London. However, in his defense, it was argued that he was only in charge of their development—Kammler directed their use. Two years after his capture, he was acquitted and offered a contract with the U.S. Air Force. Still later, in May 1950, he went into private industry as a staff member for Bell Aircraft.

Six hundred Germans were involved in Operation Backfire. Fewer than 70 were from Peenemünde, and 128 were soldiers from the Division zV. The rest were troops and civilians with no previous involvement with the V-2.

The first launch took place on 2 October 1945. Rocket #1 impacted in the North Sea just 1.9 kilometers short of the target. The second rocket, fired two days later, experienced fuel cutoff after only $34\frac{1}{2}$ seconds of powered flight and fell considerably short of its intended goal. The third and final firing of Operation Backfire was made on 15 October. This launch was attended by invited spectators, including groups from the United States, Soviet Union, France, and the press.

Meanwhile, on the other side of the Atlantic, the rocket components captured by the Americans had been delivered to the recently established White Sands Proving Ground in New Mexico.

This technological cornucopia included 215 combustion chambers, 180 sets of propellant tanks, 90 tail units, 100 sets of graphite jet vanes, and 200 turbopumps. However, it was soon discovered that Project Hermes would be plagued by some of the same problems encountered during Operation Backfire. Although there were more than adequate quantities of some components, such as tanks and combustion chambers, others, particularly control compartment hardware, were in short supply. Only 50 control gyroscopes had been shipped from Mittlewerk, most of which were in poor condition. Each rocket required two gyroscopes. Seventy electrical distribution panels were received, but many of them were without wiring.

The German rocket personnel who surrendered to the Americans were taken to Garmisch-Partenkirchen for interrogation. To utilize the experiences of the V-2 program participants, contracts to work in the United States were offered to many of the people collected at Garmisch-Partenkirchen. About a year after the V-2 was earmarked for study as part of Project Hermes, 118 German scientists and engineers who de-

German workers affix an emblem to Operation Backfire Round #1, on 1 October 1945. After two launch attempts, the rocket was removed from the launch pad, recycled and finally flown three days later (Photo courtesy of Mitchell R. Sharpe, S.I. Negative #76-9076).

Liftoff of the first Operation Backfire flight, 2 October 1945 (S.I. Negative #A 5367).

Emblem affixed to Operation Backfire Round #2. This was the first missile flown during Operation Backfire (S.I. Negative #76-9075).

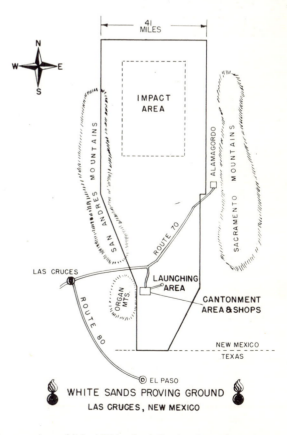

The recently established White Sands Proving Grounds near Las Cruces, New Mexico, was selected as the site for the American V-2 program, Project Hermes (S.I. Negative #80-4088).

L.B. Carter, an employee of the General Electric Company, inspects V-2 engines brought to White Sands Proving Grounds, New Mexico (S.I. Negative #79-13162).

V-2 #1 on the static test stand. This rocket was fired for 57 seconds on 15 March 1946 (S.I. Negative #80-4093).

V-2 on the launch pad at White Sands. This is an early Hermes launch, as evidenced by the use of captured German Marigus ladders and liquid oxygen trailers. Note the German liquid oxygen tank mounted on the American truck. The tower on the right was built for use with the American-designed WAC Corporal (S.I. Negative #80-4087).

Close-up of a V-2 during launch preparations at White Sands. German launch equipment is in use (S.I. Negative #80-3831).

veloped the missile arrived at Fort Bliss, Texas.

On 3 March 1946 the first V-2 prepared at White Sands was ready for firing. This rocket was not scheduled for flight; rather, V-2 #1 was taken to the static test stand for propulsion unit evaluation. Bolted securely to the massive concrete test stand, the rocket fired for 57 seconds.

The first flight occurred just over a month later, on 16 April. V-2 #2 lifted-off from the New Mexico desert at 2:47 p.m. The rocket began to fly erratically, lost a fin, and started to arc over. The engine was shut down by radio command after only 19 seconds of powered flight. Continuing to coast skyward, the missile achieved an altitude of five miles and crashed a short distance from the launch pad. After the flight it was determined that a graphite jet vane had broken off. As the rudder on the tip of the fin tried to compensate for the loss of the vane, it was subjected to unusually large flight loads which weakened the fin it was attached to.

Three weeks later, on 10 May, the first successful flight was made. Rocket #3 burned for 59 seconds before the on-board integrating accelerometer ordered thrust cutoff. The rocket then coasted to an altitude of 70 miles.

In addition to its military aspects, Project Hermes also of-fered the scientific community the opportunity to use the rocket as a vehicle to carry experiments into the upper atmo-sphere and beyond. In January 1946 the Army Ordnance De-partment held a conference for both military and university personnel to discuss the possibility of placing instruments aboard the V-2. Among the organizations represented were the Rocket Sonde Research Section of the Naval Research Laboratory and the Applied Physics Laboratory of the Johns Hopkins University. At the conference, it was explained that the goals of the Army's V-2 project were threefold: first, to gain experience in the handling and firing of large rockets; second, to obtain technical information on rocket ballistics; and third, to make measurements of the upper atmosphere. Lieutenant Colonel J.G. Bain of the Ordnance Department ex-tended a special invitation to the Rocket Sonde Research Sec-tion to participate in the upper atmosphere research phase of the program.

For the Hermes launches, of course, the explosive in the warhead was removed, leaving this volume available for in-strumentation. Both V-2s #2 and #3 used modified German-made warheads. Both carried rudimentary cosmic ray experi-ments. The nose of each rocket contained a single Geiger tube shielded by an inch-thick lead cylinder. Power for the

After the missile was raised into position on the launch pad, the gantry was rolled into place and preflight checks commenced (S.I. Negative #80-4136).

tube was supplied by an assembly of fifty-two 22.5 volt hear-ing aid batteries set in wax. In addition to the Geiger tube, each carried a roll of exposed 35-millimeter film. A gravity switch, set to function at an acceleration of four gs, was used to turn on the flight data recorder.

Unfortunately, rocket #2 failed to accelerate sufficiently

Upon completion of the prelaunch checks, the gantry was moved away from the rocket (S.I. Negative #80-4136).

The control room inside the blockhouse became a beehive of activity during a launch (S.I. Negative #79-13144).

Daniel X. Ryan, a General Electric service engineer, pushes the launch button on the firing console (S.I. Negative 13144).

Lift-off of V-2 #12 on 10 October 1946. This vehicle carried a 10-counter cosmic ray telescope, a solar spectrometer, eight 16-mm cameras for high-altitude terrain photography, and sensors to measure the temperature and pressure of the upper atmosphere. The wires extending from the fins are trailing wire antennas, which were part of an experiment to study the nature of the ionosphere. V-2 #12 reached an altitude of 102 miles (S.I. Negative #80-3827).

Even without an explosive warhead, the V-2s still made large craters when they impacted in the New Mexico desert. The remains of the missile combustion chamber is visible near the bottom of the crater. Experiment recovery after a landing such as this was impossible, so methods were devised to break apart the missiles in the air. The separate pieces descended much more slowly, and recovery of experimental equipment was possible (S.I. Negative #80-4095).

to turn on the recorder, so even though the warhead was recovered there were no data. Rocket #3 created a large crater upon impact and no trace of its warhead was ever found.

The German warheads were unsuitable for scientific work, as the casings were heavy and equipment once placed inside them was inaccessible, so new payload sections were constructed by the Naval Gun Factory in Washington, D.C. The new nose sections were made from $\frac{3}{8}$-inch thick cast steel. They contained 19.6 cubic feet of volume for payload packages. Three gasketed ports allowed access to the payload before launch. A pressure of one atmosphere was maintained inside the nose cone throughout the flight. The overall length of the new warhead was seven feet, six inches, and it weighed 1055 pounds empty.

Numerous other components, such as gyroscopes and electric junction panels, were built in the United States to German specifications. The Germans used small gauge, single strand wire in the V-2. This wire was suceptible to breakage and was finally replaced by stranded wire in 1947. Another problem encountered by the General Electric personnel preparing the captured missiles for launch was that the individual components had to be carefully inspected, cleaned, and tested before use.

Payload recovery was another technique which still had to be perfected, as evidenced by the second flight. To enhance the probability of recovering the payloads, it was proposed that the V-2 be explosively separated into two aerodynamically unstable sections before it reentered the atmosphere. If this were done, the pieces would impact at considerably slower velocities than that of an intact missile.

V-2 #5 was the first flown where a deliberate airburst was attempted. Lengths of primacord explosive were attached to the body of the missile about a foot aft the joint between the midsection and the tail. Apparently the explosive functioned and indications were that the skin of the rocket was cut by the explosive, but the plumbing which connected the propulsion unit to the mid-section held the rocket together.

On missile #6, flown on 28 June, one-pound blocks of TNT were placed on each of the four main struts of the control compartment. Following detonation, the warhead did not separate, so on V-2 #9 (flown on 30 July), one pound blocks of TNT and nitrostarch were bolted to the control compartment struts. This was sufficient to separate the nose from the rest of the rocket, and the rocket body impacted in the desert without leaving a crater. The body was in surprisingly good shape, but the warhead was another matter. Apparently the missile's nose was destroyed by the explosion, for no trace of it was ever found. On 10 October, V-2 #12 carried a two-pound piece of TNT on each strut. Separation was successful and the warhead was recovered. The next attempt was not so successful; only the baseplate of V-2 #13's warhead was found. It was badly punctured, indicating that the amount of explosive used was excessive. The next success in the attempts to explosively separate the warhead from the rest of the rocket occurred on 8 April 1947. V-2 #23 carried one-pound blocks of TNT attached to the control compartment struts immediately behind the warhead base plate. The base plate was not punctured, as with V-2 #13, but was bent in such a way to indicate that the explosive had been the cause of the separation.

Without its nose section, the body of the rocket tumbled as it fell and struck the ground at a speed of only a few hun-

Not all launches during Project Hermes were successful. Round #55 was destroyed on the pad when a special nose separation charge detonated prematurely (S.I. Negatives #77-7353, #77-7351).

dred miles per hour. After such an impact, the aft portion of missile #9 was found to be relatively undamaged, while its warhead was never found. Both V-2s, #6 and #9, carried solar spectrographs in their noses, so it was decided to place subsequent spectrographs in special housings built into the missile's fins on future missions.

V-2 #12, flown on 10 October 1946, carried a solar spectrograph in a conical housing built into fin II. This instrument was recovered and returned measurements of the solar spectrum in the ultraviolet wavelengths which are absorbed by the atmosphere. Damage to the spectrograph was so slight that it was flown again.

Seven missiles were modified for the Air Force's Blossom project. Under the aegis of the service's Cambridge Research Laboratory, the missiles' midsections were lengthened by one caliber (about 65 inches) by the Franklin Institute Laboratories for Research and Development. Larger warhead sections were added to these missiles. A standard V-2 weighed approximately 8800 pounds without propellants. The lightest Blossom vehicle weighed 9781 pounds; the heaviest, 10,683 pounds. These missiles were designed to break apart in the air and have the nose section return via parachute. Of the seven Blossom vehicles, four flew successfully.

The Navy was interested in the feasibility of launching rockets at sea. To test this, two projects, code named Pushover and Sandy were implemented. Pushover was an appropriate name for the first project—a fully fueled V-2 was toppled over to obtain data for estimating the effect of such a mishap aboard a ship.

On 6 September 1947, the first of two Operation Sandy V-2s were launched from the deck of the aircraft carrier USS Midway. The launch itself was successful but, after leaving the deck the missile went out of control, caught fire, and ex-

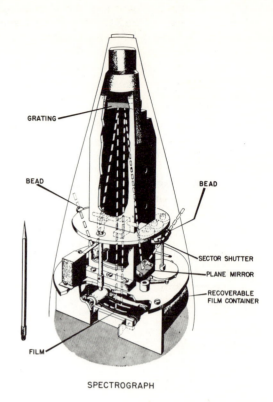

SPECTROGRAPH

Schematic of ultraviolet solar spectrograph carried in fin II of several V-2s. The lithium-fluoride bead acted as a wide-angle lens. The light beam reflects off a planar mirror and a diffraction grating and onto a roll of moving film. Spectrographs like this photographed the ultraviolet spectrum of the sun (S.I. Negative #80-2372).

V-2s on the deck of the U.S.S. Midway for Operation Sandy (S.I. Negative #80-3829).

Operation Sandy involved launching missiles from the deck of the aircraft carrier U.S.S. Midway, including this flight on 6 September 1947 (S.I. Negative #79-13145).

One of the Sandy V-2s in flight (S.I. Negative #77-6021).

ploded at an altitude of about 12,000 feet after a flight of six miles. Immediately after the launch the Midway was able to launch its aircraft. Since this test was conducted to determine whether or not a large missile could be fueled and launched from a ship which was underway and if the ship could resume normal operations immediately after launch, Operation Sandy was termed a success.

As the Hermes firings continued, scientists were provided with more and more opportunities to fly experimental packages into the upper atmosphere. Among the payloads lofted aboard V-2s were biological packages, solar spectrographs, cosmic ray telescopes, and even an experiment in which rifle grenades were used to attempt to create micrometeorites.

The first biological payload flown on a V-2 was a package of fungus spores placed aboard V-2 #17, which was launched on 17 December 1946. These spores were flown to find out if cosmic rays would cause any unusual effects on their growth and mutation. The spores were contained in five lucite cylinders placed in the missile's warhead. V-2 #17 reached an altitude of 116 miles, which was the highest altitude attained by any of the Hermes V-2s.

Corn seeds and fruit flies were also flown by researchers hoping to investigate the effects of cosmic rays on genetic mutation. The first two flights of special strains of seeds, which took place on 9 July and 19 July 1946, ended in failure when the payload on the 9 July flight was not recovered and the 19 July flight exploded 28.5 seconds into the flight. Another group of seeds were flown on V-2 #9 on 30 July 1946. The original stock of seeds supplied by Harvard University had been exhausted. After two recovery failures, little hope was held for the possibility of recovering the payload after the flight, so a package of ordinary corn seeds was purchased in nearby Las Cruces, New Mexico, for the experiment. As luck would have it, V-2 #9 reached an altitude of 104 miles and the seeds, located in pouches inside the rocket's body, were recovered. A later V-2 carried fruit flies in containers which were ejected from the rocket. A ribbon parachute deployed upon ejection slowed the container and allowed a larger parachute to open when the container had descended to an altitude of 100,000 feet. The insects were successfully recovered.

On the morning of 11 June 1948, a nine-pound Rhesus monkey named Albert was placed in a sealed capsule aboard V-2 #37. The monkey, which was anesthetized, apparently suffocated before the rocket was launched. In any event, he would not have survived the landing after the capsule's recovery system malfunctioned.

Improvements were made in the capsule's design, and another Rhesus, Albert II, was placed aboard missile #47, flown on 14 June 1949. The rocket attained an altitude of 83 miles, and telemetry indicated the monkey survived until impact, for the recovery system again failed.

Two more primate flights were made, one of which exploded in mid-air. The last attempt to fly a monkey on a V-2 ended with another parachute failure. One final biological payload was flown aboard the German rockets launched from WSPG. In the summer of 1950, a mouse was placed in a capsule equipped with a camera to record the rodent's reaction to acceleration and weightlessness. Again, the recovery system failed, but the camera survived.

One of the more unusual series of experiments to be carried aboard the V-2 was flown in late 1946, when attempts were made to create micrometeorites using rifle grenades. It was calculated that the velocity of the jet from a standard shaped-charge rifle grenade was comparable to the lower range of meteor velocities. It was hoped that if grenades of this type were ejected and detonated at a high enough altitude, artificial meteors would be produced. Since the mass, velocity, and composition of the ejected matter was known, data from this experiment would aid scientists in their measurements of natural meteors; the experiment would also yield data on the physical properties of the upper atmosphere.

The first experiment in the series was flown aboard V-2 #12 on 24 October 1946. Black powder charges were substituted for the rifle grenades to test the grenade ejection equipment. As an added bonus from this test, it was predicted that the smoke puffs from the charges would provide a method for studying air currents at high altitudes. The equipment operated as planned and the charges were detonated at altitudes of about 100,000, 160,000, and 200,000 feet. However, the black powder did not give the hoped-for discrete smoke puffs; rather it resulted in smoke streamers indicating that there were high winds aloft, but which could not be used to quantify the conclusions.

One of the more innovative experiments to be carried out was an attempt on V-2 #17 (launched 17 December 1946) to create micrometeorites. Here (left to right) John Adderson, Louis Padderson (both from the New Mexico School of Mines), Lt. Col. Harold R. Turner (Commander of White Sands Proving Ground), Dr. James Van Allen, and Arthur Coyne (both from Johns Hopkins University) discuss an experiment that involved launching M-7 rifle grenades from a V-2 in flight (S.I. Negative #80-4733).

Lt. Col. Harold R. Turner installs the M-7 rifle grenades aboard V-2 #17 (S.I. Negative #80-3835).

Modified M-7 rifle grenades were placed aboard V-2 #17, which was launched at 10:12 p.m. MST on 17 December 1946. One observer reported seeing a streak of light originating from the rocket, but he was the only one who saw anything. Postflight analysis indicated that the grenade ejection mechanism probably failed. Subsequent tests showed that the jet from an M-7 grenade was too weak for this application anyway.

Beginning in 1948 a smaller rocket, the WAC Corporal, was placed on top of the V-2 to create a two-stage vehicle. Eight of these "Project Bumper" vehicles were flown between 1948 and 1950. An altitude record of 244 miles was set by Bumper 5 on 24 February 1949. After being boosted to a velocity of 3800 feet per second by the V-2, the WAC Corporal's engine propelled the 16-foot rocket to a final speed of 7480 feet per second.

Bumper 8 was launched on 24 July 1950, five days before Bumper 7, whose flight was postponed due to technical problems. These were the first launches from the Eastern Test Range at Cape Canaveral, Florida.

The last two Project Bumper launches took place at Cape Canaveral, Florida. The lighthouse in the background is still a familiar landmark at the Cape (S.I. Negative #77-4220).

On 24 July 1950 Bumper #8 became the first rocket launched from the Eastern Test Range at Cape Canaveral, Florida. Technical difficulties postponed the flight of Bumper #7 until 29 July (S.I. Negative #76-15532).

Launch of Bumper #7 (S.I. Negative #80-2368).

A small American-built rocket, the WAC Corporal, was placed on top of the V-2 to create a two-stage vehicle during Project Bumper. This vehicle, Bumper #5, set an altitude record of 244 miles on 24 February 1949. Eight Bumper rockets were flown (S.I. Negative #79-13157).

When the General Electric Company's participation in the V-2 program ended on 30 June 1951, 67 rockets had been fired as a part of Project Hermes. Unlike Operation Backfire, where German personnel prepared and launched rockets under British observation, Project Hermes was intended from the outset to be primarily an American effort. The number of German personnel at WSPG reached its peak of 39 in March 1946. Thereafter, the German specialists were replaced with General Electric personnel. By the spring of 1947, this had been completed.

The end of the V-2 phase of Hermes was not the end of the American V-2 launches. The White Sands launches had been supported by personnel of the U.S. Army's 1st Guided Missile Battalion, formed on 11 October 1945. After the Hermes V-2 firings were concluded, the 1st Guided Missile Battalion fired three V-2s. The first of these, TF-1, was launched on 22 August 1951. Its engine fired until all propellants were consumed, in a test to see how high an altitude could be achieved by a six-year-old German rocket launched by American soldiers. TF-1 reached an altitude of 132 miles, the highest ever attained by a V-2.

After the supply of captured German rockets was exhausted, the roar of rocket motors could still be heard rumbling across the New Mexico Desert. The U.S. Navy had been flying its own rocket, the Viking, since 1949. Other American rockets such as the Aerobee and WAC Corporal were also being flown from White Sands. The German rocket specialists who built the A-4 continued their work—this time for the U.S. Army. As they designed larger rockets, the group drew upon the wealth of knowledge gained while building the A-4 at Peenemünde. Working alongside the Germans were Americans, many of whom received their first practical engineering experience with the V-2s at White Sands.

The V-2 led to the Redstone and Jupiter ballistic missiles. These begat the Saturn series—first the Saturn I, then the Saturn IB, then finally the mammoth Saturn V which launched Apollo astronauts to the moon. Alongside a 364-foot Saturn V, the 26-foot A-4 is miniscule, yet it is the grandfather of the large rockets of today. As such, it formed the technological base from which we entered the space age.

TF-1 was the first V-2 launched by the First Guided Missile Battalion on 22 August 1951. This missile reached an altitude of 132 miles, the highest ever attained by a V-2 (S.I. Negative #77-1012).

V-2 on the launch pad at White Sands Proving Ground (S.I. Negative #80-3830).

Appendix 1:
A Technical Description of the A-4

The following is a brief description of the A-4 missile and the operation of its internal components. This description is far from comprehensive; the A-4 was a complicated machine with many thousands of parts. Rather, the missile has been broken down into its five major subassemblies: warhead, control compartment, mid-section, propulsion unit, and tail unit, each of which is described to give the reader an overall picture of the internal mechanisms of the first long-range liquid-fuel rocket.

a. Warhead

The A-4 carried a high explosive warhead with an impact-detonating fuse system. Despite its relatively simple construction when compared to the rest of the rocket, a considerable amount of work was required to develop a satisfactory warhead. When the payload for the A-4 was first being designed, several conflicting requirements had to be met. The explosive had to be as powerful as possible yet be insensitive to shock and heat so it would not detonate during launch or reentry. The fuses had similar constraints—they had to be sensitive enough to detonate the warhead just at impact so it would not bury itself first and reduce the power of the explosion, but they had to withstand a 6 g[1] acceleration and the vibrations created during powered flight.

Amatol, a mixture of 60 percent TNT and 40 percent ammonium nitrate, was selected as the high-explosive that offered the best combination of brisance (shattering effect) and insensitivity to shock and heat. Also, it could be cast with a minimum of difficulty.

The filling was placed in a 2 m long ogive made from sheet steel 6 mm thick. This casing provided an aerodynamic shroud for the explosive and a structure for the warhead components. Initially, the A-4 was planned to carry one metric ton (2200 pounds) of high explosive, but preliminary calculations showed this would have to be the total warhead weight if a range of 160 miles was to be attained by the missile. The warhead casing weighed 550 pounds, leaving 1650 pounds for the Amatol.

Two fuses were used: one in the warhead's nose, the other in its base. The nose fuse, designated KZ-3, contained two inertia switches perpendicular to one another and a crushable dome switch. When the dome switch struck the ground, its inner and outer shells made contact to close the firing circuit. The perpendicular inertia switches were set to function if either a target impact or graze occurred. As a back-up to the nose fuse another fuse, BZ-3, was located in the base of the warhead. It did not have a crushable switch, but was otherwise identical in construction and operation to the KZ-3 fuse. A silica cap over the top of the KZ-3 protected the dome switch from damage prior to impact. Actuation of any one of the five switches in the two fuses was sufficient to initiate the explosive train and detonate the warhead.

The fuses were armed by a two-switch system. The first switch was controlled by the event timer in the control compartment and was closed 40 seconds after launch. Switch two was closed when the engine's thrust stopped, about 60 seconds into the flight. Operated in this sequence, the two switches armed the warhead fuses. If the propulsion unit malfunctioned and the second switch closed first, the fuses were deactivated, preventing normal warhead detonation on impact. This was intended as a safety feature for the benefit of

The conical nose fuse and circular base fuse. Both fuses were packaged and shipped together (S.I. Negative #80-2363).

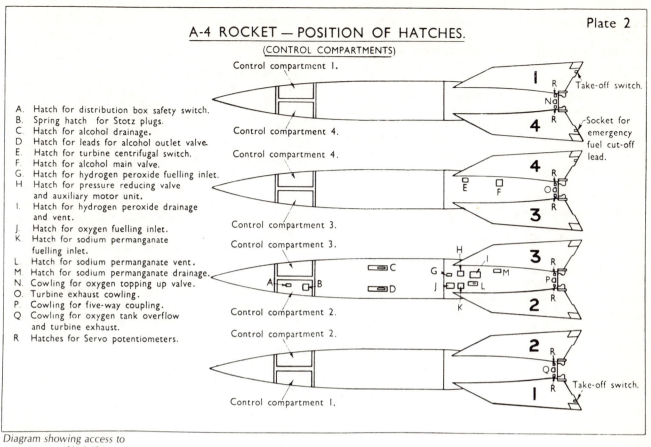

A-4 ROCKET — POSITION OF HATCHES.
(CONTROL COMPARTMENTS)

Plate 2

A. Hatch for distribution box safety switch.
B. Spring hatch for Stotz plugs.
C. Hatch for alcohol drainage.
D. Hatch for leads for alcohol outlet valve.
E. Hatch for turbine centrifugal switch.
F. Hatch for alcohol main valve.
G. Hatch for hydrogen peroxide fuelling inlet.
H. Hatch for pressure reducing valve and auxiliary motor unit.
I. Hatch for hydrogen peroxide drainage and vent.
J. Hatch for oxygen fuelling inlet.
K. Hatch for sodium permanganate fuelling inlet.
L. Hatch for sodium permanganate vent.
M. Hatch for sodium permanganate drainage.
N. Cowling for oxygen topping up valve.
O. Turbine exhaust cowling.
P. Cowling for five-way coupling.
Q. Cowling for oxygen tank overflow and turbine exhaust.
R. Hatches for Servo potentiometers.

Diagram showing access to components of V-2 (S.I. Negative #70-13187).

Cutaway of the warhead (S.I. Negative #79-13174).

THE WARHEAD

Plate 3.

Silica cap
Nose fuze
Exploder tube
Alcohol pressurising pipe
Amatol
Base fuze

the launching personnel in case of an impact in the launch area. However, there were several crashes in which the warhead detonated anyway, due to the violence of the impacts. The reliability of the fusing system was excellent; only two unexploded warheads were found during the war.

A small primer charge, designated F 36, was contained in each fuse. The primer initiated the detonator, contained in a tube 3.5 cm in diameter along the axis of the warhead. This tube was filled with Penthrite and was connected to the fuses at either end. Upon impact the fuses detonated the primers, which set off the detonator, causing the main charge to explode.

About 1 m off the nose tip there was an opening in the side of the warhead casing. A 6 cm pipe extended from this opening to the base of the warhead, where it connected to another pipe in the control compartment via a brass bellows. This pipe continued through the control compartment to the top of the alcohol tank. Air entering the port on the side of the warhead was used to pressurize the alcohol tank. This prevented the tank from collapsing as it was emptied and also helped the fuel pump. The total weight of the warhead, with its 16.7 cubic feet of Amatol, was 1000 kilograms (2204 pounds).

b. Control Compartment

The control compartment, a truncated ogive just below the warhead, contained the mechanisms that directed the A-4 during its powered flight. Guidance and control of the missile proved to be among the most crucial problems facing the team at Peenemünde, for if the A-4 was to become an effective weapon it had to be able to strike its target accurately.

The trajectory of the rocket had two phases: powered and ballistic. Control was exercised over the missile only during the powered phase. After engine cutoff it followed a ballistic trajectory like any other artillery shell.

All rockets were assumed to follow the same trajectory during powered flight. Four seconds after launch, the rocket began a preprogrammed pitch toward the target until an angle of 47° was reached about 43 seconds into the flight. After this, the elevation angle was held constant and the rocket continued to accelerate until the velocity necessary to achieve the desired range was attained.

Two methods of controlling engine cutoff were used. The first was to terminate the thrust by ground command via radio. The other was to have a device on board the rocket that could determine the velocity and issue the cutoff signal at the proper time.

Radio-control cutoff proved to be the most accurate, but offered several disadvantages. There was always a fear that

External view of the control compartment (S.I. Negative #79-2363).

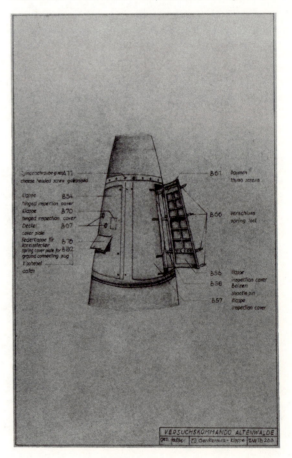

1. The term g refers to the acceleration of gravity, approximately 9.8 meters per second per second. Hence 6 g would result in an acceleration of 58.8 meters per second per second.

the Allies would jam the control signal. It was also feared that the additional vehicles required for the radio equipment would present a more appealing target for Allied air attack. Finally, there was the logistical burden of maintaining additional equipment and vehicles. Despite these disadvantages, this method was used with increased frequency toward the end of the war due to the higher accuracy.

On-board equipment for radio control consisted of a receiver-transmitter called Verdoppler or Ortley, and a control receiver called Honnef. The Verdoppler received signals on a frequency of 30.7 megacycles and retransmitted on 61.4 megacycles. The retransmitted signal was compared to the second harmonic of the one transmitted from the ground. A beat frequency proportional to the rocket's velocity was produced due to the Doppler effect.

The Honnef consisted of a superhetrodyne receiver, an audio-frequency filter unit, a relay unit, and a three-phase power supply. This receiver was used to first reduce the fuel supply to the propellant turbopump and then stop it altogether. It was found that after the cutoff signal was sent to a rocket firing at the full 25-ton thrust it took 2.7 seconds for the thrust to reach zero, which had an adverse effect on the accuracy of the round. Because of this, a two-step engine cut-off was used. When the rocket reached 95 percent of its desired velocity, engine thrust was reduced to eight tons, and terminated when final velocity was attained. This two-step engine cutoff reduced dispersion errors by as much as 50 percent.

An antijam device which used a combination of modulated tones, called Kommandogerät, was used. The receiver had a narrow-band filter as an added measure against jamming of the signal. Even more elaborate mechanisms, such as a panoramic search receiver, were planned in the event of any difficulties being encountered. There were no incidents of Allied jamming of the control signal, so these devices were not used.

As an alternate means of thrust cutoff control, integrating accelerometers were developed. Of the rockets fired against England, 90 percent used these devices. The integrating accelerometer determined the velocity of the rocket as a function of acceleration. When the proper velocity was achieved, thrust was terminated in the same two-step manner as with the radio control method. Two types of integrating accelerometer were used; a torque balance accelerometer with an electrolytic integrator and a gyroscopic type with an accelerometer and integrator.

The torque balance accelerometer was developed by Professors Theodor Buchold and Carl Wagner at the Technische Hochschule, Darmstadt. It consisted of a device to deliver a direct current proportional to the acceleration, and an electrolytic cell which integrated the current with respect to time.

The electrolytic cell contained two silver electrodes and an electrolyte solution containing sodium chloride, acetic acid, and sodium acetate. Proportions of the chemicals were 15 grams of sodium chloride, 60 grams of acetic acid, and 136 grams of sodium acetate per liter of solution.

During manufacture, one of the electrodes was heavily coated with silver chloride. To prepare the cell for use and program it for a desired cutoff velocity, the normal polarity of the cell was reversed so that the coated electrode was negative. With the flow of current reversed, the torque balance produced a current proportional to the Earth's gravitational acceleration, g_o. Current was allowed to pass through the

cell for a time period, t_o, such that the product of g_o and t_o equaled the desired cutoff velocity ($g_o \times t_o = V_c$). As current passed through the cell, chloride ions moved to the previously uncoated electrode and formed a layer of silver chloride on the anode. At the end of the timed period the original connections were restored and the cell was ready for use.

During flight, a current proportional to the rocket's acceleration was supplied by the torque balance accelerometer. The accelerometer contained a mass attached to a lever arm which developed a torque proportional to the acceleration perpendicular to the arm. The pivot of the lever arm carried a galvanometer coil which moved in the field of a permanent magnet. Current through this coil produced a torque. As long as the magnet-generated torque just compensated for the acceleration-produced torque in the lever arm, the coil current was exactly proportional to the acceleration.

To produce and control the coil current necessary to compensate for the accelerative forces on the lever arm, the mass on the end of the arm (a copper disc) was used with two iron-core inductive coils to form an inductive pick-up sensitive to minute movements of the lever. The inductive coils formed two sides of an inductance bridge. The other two sides were formed by the two halves of the center-tapped primary winding of a grid circuit transformer in the amplifier unit. Movement by the lever arm from its zero position advanced the copper disc into one air gap and extracted it from the other. This charged the impedance of the inductive coils and created an imbalance in the bridge. Output from the bridge was rectified and amplified to produce the current needed to balance the torque generated by the acceleration.

During flight, as the current flowed through the electrolytic cells, the freshly deposited silver chloride was transferred to the original electrode. When the transfer of silver chloride was complete, a sharp rise in cell voltage occurred. This was the signal that the rocket had accelerated long enough to reach the preprogrammed desired velocity, and triggered the thrust control relays. Each accelerometer contained two electrolytic cells. Preflight programming was first started in one cell. About 20 seconds later the second cell was placed in series with the first. During flight the second cell (with the smaller amount of silver chloride on the anode) was used to control thrust reduction, while the signal from the first cell controlled final engine cutoff when the exact velocity was reached.

Temperature fluctuations affect the solubility of silver chloride, and adversely affected the accuracy of the cell. To counter this, the cells were placed into an insulated container with a bimetallic heater, which maintained the temperature of the cell at 35° C. It was claimed that these integrating accelerometers produced thrust cutoff velocities to within 0.1 percent of the desired values.

The gyroscopic integrating accelerometer contained an electrically driven gyroscope suspended from a gimbal which was perpendicular to the axis of rotation of its rotor. The gimbal was balanced and pivoted about an axis parallel to the longitudinal axis of the rocket. Because of this arrangement, an acceleration along the rocket's longitudinal axis caused the gyroscope to precess about the gimbal's pivot axis. The angle of precession was proportional to the integral with respect to time of the acceleration, or more simply, the velocity.

Through a series of reduction gears, the gimbal drove a wheel which had three contacts on it. The first contact indi-

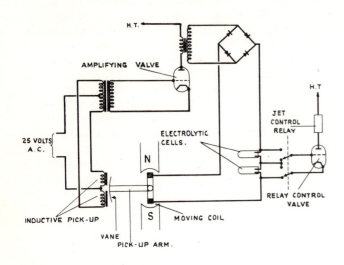

SIMPLIFIED WORKING DIAGRAM OF SINGLE
STAGE ELECTROLYTIC INTEGRATING
ACCELEROMETER.

The gyroscopic integrating accelerometer. The gyroscope is visible on the right side of the assembly, below the large gear and wheel which contained the contacts to order fuel cutoff. The two knobs on top of the accelerometer were used to program the device for the desired cutoff velocity. This specimen is from the collection of the National Air and Space Museum (S.I. Negative #79-13370-73).

cated the starting point at liftoff, the second was used for thrust reduction, and the third for controlled thrust termination.

Each of the latter two contacts could be set by remote control to any point on the wheel during prelaunch preparations. The angular separation of these contacts was adjustable in tenth of a degree increments over a 360° range.

Under laboratory conditions, the gyroscopic integrating accelerometer had a measured accuracy of 0.1 percent. In the field, under operational conditions, the accuracy was about 0.3–0.4 percent. Minor variations in the gyroscope rotors were the primary cause for these errors.

The control compartment was divided into four quadrants by radial plywood sheets. Radio control equipment occupied the first quadrant. Also in quadrant I were the batteries, which supplied power to the rocket's electrical components. Two 27.5 volt lead-acid batteries with eight cells each connected in series were the main power source. These batteries provided 27 volts with 20 ampere discharge for about five minutes. Both batteries were designed to withstand an acceleration of 6 g and to function in any position.

Quadrant II housed the sequence switch, main distribution panel, and fuse arming unit.

The sequence switch controlled functions of the rocket which had to occur at a specific time, and in a definite order. It consisted of an electric-motor driven cam shaft which operated a number of contacts. Two types of switches were used. In the earlier version, all of the cams were on a common shaft powered by a conventional series-wound electric motor. A smaller version with the cams mounted on two separate shafts driven by a ratchet-type motor was introduced later.

Contacts in the sequence switch controlled the radio

Internal sequencing was controlled by a timer. This is the single-shaft type. Later models of the A-4 used a sequencer switch, which used cams mounted on two shafts driven by a ratchet motor. This specimen is in the collection of the National Air and Space Museum (S.I. Negative #79-13370-32).

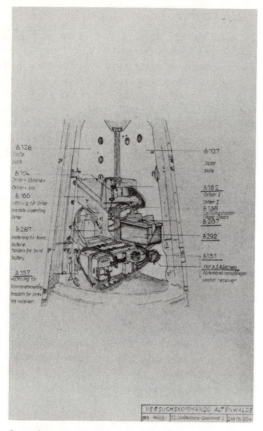

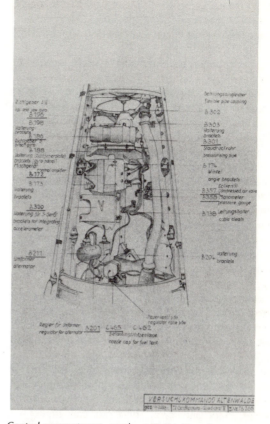

Control compartment, quadrant I (S.I. Negative #79-13211).

Control compartment, quadrant III (S.I. Negative #79-13195).

Control compartment, quadrant II (S.I. Negative #79-13212).

Control compartment, quadrant IV (S.I. Negative #79-13192).

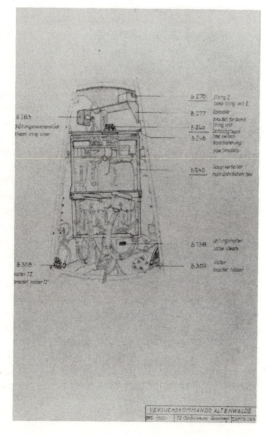

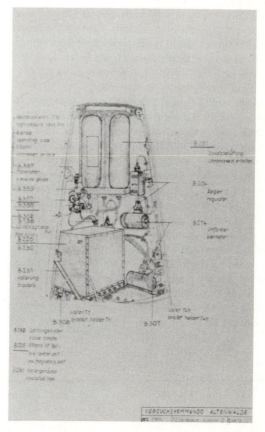

equipment, horizontal gyroscope, alcohol tank pressurizing valve, and the warhead arming unit. As a back-up to the other fuel cutoff devices, a contact was used to signal cutoff 65 seconds after launch.

The main distribution panel provided a single location for concentrating and cross-connecting leads from the steering controls in the control compartment to the steering mechanisms located in the tail unit. There were two ground-connecting plugs which were the interface between the rocket's electrical circuits and ground test equipment. Electrical power distribution to the various systems was also controlled by the main distribution panel.

The fuse arming unit contained the double-switch arrangement (described in the warhead section) that armed the warhead fuses.

The third quadrant contained the integrating accelerometer, pitch gyroscope, roll and yaw gyroscope, control amplifier, voltage regulator and alternator, 50 volt signal battery, and the alcohol tank pressurizing pipe and valve assembly. The pitch gyroscope directed the rocket during the preprogrammed powered phase of the flight. A single gyroscope was used to detect motions in both the yaw and roll axes. If any such movements were measured, signals were sent to the steering mechanisms in the rocket tail unit. Both gyroscopes were essentially the same, with the rotors being driven by a three-phase 500-cycle power supply. Rotor speed was just under 30,000 revolutions per minute. The primary difference between the two was the addition of a small motor, called the program motor, to the pitch gyro. This motor consisted of a ratchet-driven wheel that rotated a small cam shaft through a worm drive. The ratchet was driven by an electric magnet energized by an interrupted direct current. During flight, the program motor cam shaft rotated slowly and in turn rotated the housing of the pick-up potentiometer. Signals from the potentiometer were sent to the pitch rudders, causing the rocket to tilt toward its target. Current for the potentiometers in the control gyroscopes was supplied by a 21-cell nickel cadmium signal battery, which had a voltage of 50 volts and a discharge rate of 300 milliamperes for five minutes.

An azimuth-control device called Viktoria Leitstrahl was contained in the fourth quadrant, along with several compressed air bottles for pressurizing the alcohol tank. The Viktoria Leitstrahl was a "beam-riding" device. A radio beam was continuously transmitted to the rocket from a ground station. If any deviation from the center of the beam was detected, a corrective signal was sent to the steering mechanism in the tail unit. Developed by the Lorenz Company, the Viktoria Leitstrahl was used mostly on later versions of the A-4.

Forty seconds after launch, the valve in the alcohol tank pressurizing pipe closed. After this action, pressure for the tank was supplied by three compressed air cylinders in the fourth quadrant. Each cylinder had a capacity of seven liters, and a working pressure of 200 atmospheres.

Total weight of the control compartment was 461 kilograms (1025 pounds).

c. Midsection

The missile midsection consisted of the alcohol tank, liquid oxygen tank, and body shell. Within the tanks, there were also numerous valves to control the flow of propellants.

A semi-monocoque structure with a sheet steel skin attached to strengthening ribs and stringers was used for the body shell, which was split lengthwise into two halves. One of the halves had two rectangular covers for access to the alcohol tank drainage valve and outlets. The other half had two ports to allow equalization of the interior and exterior pressures during flight. The skin was spot-welded to the ribs. For added strength (needed because of the airburst problem), a second layer of skin was riveted to the forward portion of the midsection shell.

The body shell also supported the propellant tanks, which were made from a light-weight aluminum-magnesium alloy. Inside the shell, the B-stoff, or alcohol, tank was mounted forward of the A-stoff (liquid oxygen) tank. When the body shell was assembled, a 110 mm wide fairing covered the seams between the halves.

The alcohol tank tapered toward the nose of the rocket. It held 9200 pounds of fuel and had a volume of 183 cubic feet. The thickness of the metal used for the sides and top was 1.2 mm; the bottom, 2 mm. The tank sections were welded together. Horizontal strengthening ribs were spot-welded inside the tank. The alcohol inlet valve was located on the forward end of the tank. Also on the forward end was the connection for the pressurizing pipe which extended through the control compartment and warhead. At the base of the tank was an outlet valve and a drainage valve. The outlet valve was connected via a bellows connection to the fuel delivery pipe, which extended through a conduit in the liquid oxygen tank to the alcohol pump.

Like the alcohol tank, the liquid oxygen tank was made from an aluminum-magnesium alloy. Four 2 mm thick pieces were used to fabricate the tank. Six strengthening ribs were spot-welded to the inside of the tank. Tank capacity was 12,200 pounds of liquid oxygen, with a volume of 170 cubic feet. The tank was filled via a 66.5 mm diameter pipe located in the base. The main delivery pipe, also located in the base of the tank, was 145 mm in diameter. As the rocket sat on the launch pad, some of the cryogenic liquid oxygen ($-186°$ C.) boiled off. To ensure an adequate supply of oxidizer when the rocket was launched, a special inlet was provided to top off the tank immediately prior to launch. If launched at the scheduled time, topping off was unnecessary. However, under tactical conditions, delays were not uncommon, so provisions for replacing the liquid oxygen which boiled off were required. Experience showed that the rocket would lose about 4.4 pounds (2 kg) of liquid oxygen per minute while awaiting launch.

Glass wool insulation was placed between the tanks and body shell. This was an expedient solution to the airburst problem discovered during the Heidelager firing trials. It seemed to work; the rate of failures was cut in half, so it was adopted as a standard feature of the rocket.

A bulkhead at the base of the midsection separated it from the propulsion unit. It was a three-piece sheet-metal circular plate with a flanged rim. The bulkhead prevented any small fires which might have developed in the tail unit from fuel leakage or spillage from damaging the tanks. Air

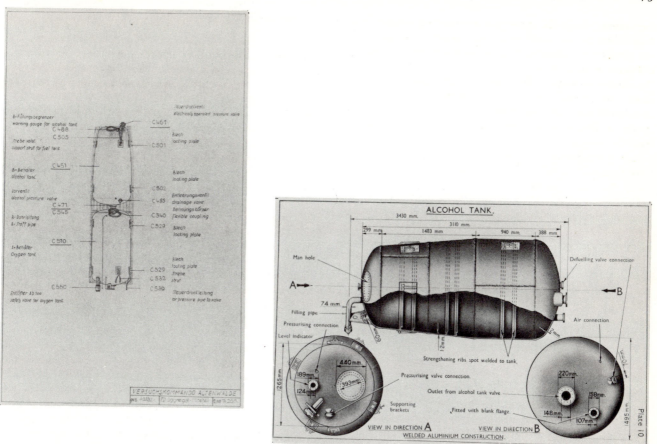

Cutaway view and diagrams of the missile midsection (S.I. Negatives #79-13204, #79-13175, #79-13176).

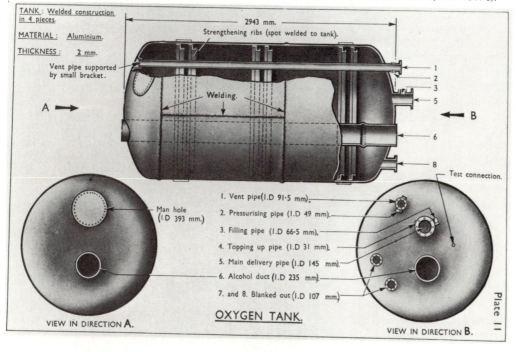

movement through the missile due to its high speed was also blocked by the bulkhead. These drafts could cause cooling in the propulsion unit and reduce engine performance. A layer of insulation was placed over the bulkhead, between it and the liquid oxygen tank. There were five openings in the bulkhead for plumbing connections between the midsection, tail unit, and propulsion unit, as well as four hand-holds equally spaced along the outer rim. The hand-holds had spring-loaded covers.

The total weight of the midsection was 742 kilograms (1640 pounds).

The thousands of small nozzles that atomized the propellants are visible in this view of the combustion chamber head (S.I. Negative #80-2373).

d. *Propulsion Section*

The propulsion section can be sub-divided into three assemblies: the combustion chamber, the turbopump, and the steam generator. As its name implies, the combustion chamber is where the propellants were combined and burned. The combustion products escaped through a nozzle at the chamber's base to generate the motor's thrust. A steam-powered turbopump supplied propellants to the combustion chamber.

The combustion chamber consisted of two sections: the head and lower section. Both sections were made of steel. The head contained 18 propellant injectors and the main alcohol inlet, while the lower section formed the de Laval nozzle, which accelerated and expelled the combustion products.

Each of the 18 cup-shaped injectors had an inlet pipe at its top for liquid oxygen. The injectors were arranged in a pattern of two concentric circles: twelve in the outer circle, six in the inner one. A single large inlet for alcohol extended from the center of the chamber top. Each injector housed rows of small nozzles, which atomized the propellants. Altogether, there were 2160 nozzles for the liquid oxygen and 1224 for the alcohol.

The combustion chamber was built with an inner and an outer wall. Alcohol circulated through the space between the two walls to cool the chamber. This technique, called regenerative cooling, is still used in rocket engines today. Near the base of the lower section there were six inlets through which the alcohol for engine cooling entered. As an added measure of protection from the heat of combustion, four horizontal rows of holes were drilled in the inner wall of the chamber.

These holes were filled with a low-melting-point metal (Wood's metal, which melts at 60° C). When the engine ignited, these plugs melted and alcohol seeped through the holes to form a protective cooling film along the nozzle wall.

In early liquid-fuel rockets such as the A-2, A-3, and A-5, propellants were forced out of the tanks by gas pressure. For a rocket the size of the A-4, tanks to withstand the necessary pressures would have been too heavy for flight, so propellants were pump-fed to the combustion chamber. The turbopump consisted of a steam turbine with two rotary pumps mounted on either side. The turbine was attached directly to the shaft of the alcohol pump, while an elastic pin coupling connected it to the oxygen pump. Both pump shafts were aligned with a journal.

Liquid oxygen reacts violently with organic materials, so oilless bearings were used in the oxygen pump. A small amount of the oxidizer was forced onto the bearings to form a lubricating film of oxygen between the shaft and the bearings.

The turbine wheel had two sets of bucket-like blades on each side of the outer edge. High-temperature steam from the steam generator impinged first on the oxygen-side of the turbine, then on the alcohol side. The blades on the alcohol-pump side of the wheel were larger than those on the oxygen side to allow for cooling, expansion, and subsequent pressure drop of the steam. The turbine developed 460 horsepower with a rotation of 3800 revolutions per minute. An overspeed cutoff was attached to the alcohol pump shaft. If the turbine reached a speed of 4500 revolutions per minute, the steam supply to the wheel was interrupted to prevent damage to the rocket.

The spiral-shell rotary pumps mounted on either side of the turbine delivered the propellants to the combustion chamber at a pressure of 18 atmospheres, about 3 atmospheres greater than chamber pressure during firing. Actual output pressures from the pumps were different: 23 atmospheres for the alcohol pump, 17.5 atmospheres for the other. The liquid oxygen pressure increased slightly on its way from the pump to the combustion chamber while the alcohol, which had a longer path to the injectors (through the space between the combustion chamber walls), decreased in pressure. An aluminum-silicon alloy, called Silumin Gamma, was used for the pump impellers and housings. The turbopump weighed 159 kg (350 pounds).

Steam for the turbopump was created from catalytic decomposition of hydrogen peroxide (H_2O_2). The hydrogen peroxide, or T-Stoff, was held in an egg-shaped steel tank. The tank held up to 132 liters of 82 percent hydrogen peroxide. A 27 percent solution of sodium permanganate ($NaMnO_4$), called Z-Stoff, was used as the catalyst to decompose the peroxide. The Z-Stoff tank had a volume of 11 liters. Both tanks were protected against corrosion inside and out by a layer of aluminum-bronze alloy.

The two chemicals were combined in a mixing chamber, and the resultant chemical reaction produced steam, oxygen, and manganese dioxide at a temperature of 385° C. Both the peroxide and the permanganate were forced out of their tanks by air pressure supplied by an assembly of seven high-pressure steel flasks called the P-Battery. Each flask had a volume of seven liters and a working pressure of 200 atmospheres. The P-Battery was connected to a pressure reduction valve which reduced the pressure from 200 atmospheres to 30 atmospheres. In addition to pressurizing the T-Stoff and Z-

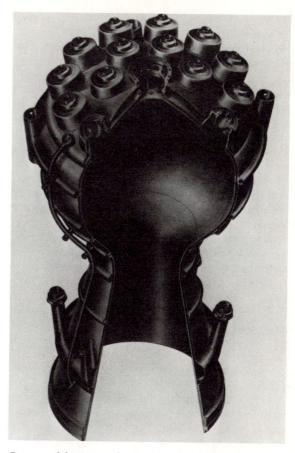

Cutaway of the A-4 combustion chamber showing injection cups, double-wall construction, and rows of orifices for film-cooling of the nozzle (S.I. Negative #79-1636).

The egg-shaped hydrogen peroxide tank can be clearly seen in this view of the propulsion section steam unit. Sodium permanganate was contained in the cylindrical tank at the base of the unit (S.I. Negative #79-13566).

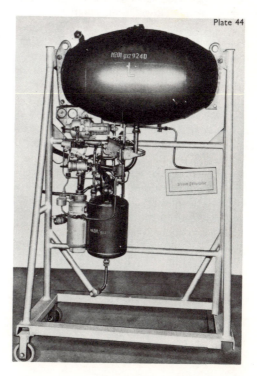

Plate 44

Stoff tanks, the P-Battery also provided pressure to operate the missile's pneumatic valves during flight.

As steam exhausted from the turbopump, it passed through a heat exchanger. The heat exchanger consisted of four sets of tubular coils. Liquid oxygen flowed through the coils after the rocket reached main stage while the turbine exhaust, with a temperature of 280° C passed over the coils. The liquid oxygen in the coils vaporized and formed gaseous oxygen under pressure. The gaseous oxygen was then ducted back into the liquid oxygen tank with a pressure of about 1.3 atmospheres. Pressurization helped force the oxidizer out of the tank and prevented it from collapsing as it was emptied.

After passing through the heat exchanger, steam exhausted from the base of the rocket via two outlets located between fins I and II, and fins III and IV.

During the first few seconds after ignition, propellants were gravity-fed to the combustion chamber. This was called the preliminary stage and allowed the firing officer to observe combustion before committing the vehicle to flight. Preliminary stage thrust was about 2.5 tons. After determining that the combustion chamber was functioning properly, the firing officer ordered the rocket's main stage, or full thrust. The 25-ton valve was opened which allowed hydrogen peroxide to enter the mixing chamber and activated the turbopump. Engine thrust quickly built up to 25.7 tons, and the rocket lifted off.

The three subassemblies of the propulsion section were mounted on a tubular steel frame of four longerons, two rectangular braces, five diagonal struts, and two circular formers. Each longeron was attached to one end to the top of the combustion chamber and to the base of the midsection on the other. These members transmitted the force of the engine's thrust to the body of the missile.

When the rocket reached 95 percent of the desired velocity, thrust was reduced to eight tons to reduce its acceleration so more precise control could be exercised over the final cut-off velocity. When thrust reduction was ordered, the 25-ton valve in the steam generator closed, while another valve, the eight-ton valve, remained open. The eight-ton valve reduced the amount of hydrogen peroxide reaching the mixing chamber, reducing the amount of steam produced. Thus, a reduced quantity of propellants was pumped to the combustion chamber and thrust was reduced. The eight-ton valve was closed, which halted the operation of the turbopump, when thrust termination was desired.

During the preliminary stage, the A-4 consumed about 38 kg of liquid oxygen and 35 kg of alcohol per second. These quantities increased to 72 kg and 58 kg per second, respectively, during main stage. The propulsion unit weighed 931 kg (2050 pounds). Engine thrust was 252,000 newtons (56,600 pounds). The temperature inside the combustion chamber during firing reached 2000° C. and the velocity of the engine's exhaust was about 2000 m per second.

e. Tail Unit

The missile tail unit consisted of an ogival boat tail with four fins. The boat tail provided an aerodynamic fairing over the propulsion unit while the fins supported the rocket on the launch pad and stabilized it during flight. Control surfaces (jet vanes and rudders) along with their servo and electric motors were also contained in the tail unit.

Construction of the boat tail was similar to that of the midsection. A skin of sheet steel was spot-welded to longerons and supported by circular formers. The longerons, or longitudinal ribs, stiffened the body lengthwise. Formers furnished cross-bracing for the boat tail. Additionally, the ribs of the fins were attached to the formers. A ribbed former at the base of the boat tail projected into the fins and was the attachment point for the tail ring.

The tail unit attached to the midsection by the former on its top. When the two sections were bolted together, a 5 mm gap existed between them to allow for ventilation in the tail.

Jet vanes and aerodynamic rudders controlled the rocket during powered flight. The jet vanes were placed in the exhaust jet of the rocket motor. Movement of the vanes deflected the exhaust and caused the rocket to rotate about one of its three axes. The vanes on fins I and III controlled the rocket's pitch. The other pair controlled yaw and roll. A rudder was incorporated into the outer-most tip of each fin. The rudders on fins II and IV were linked to the servo motors that operated the jet vanes by a sprocket and chain, and were used to control yaw and roll. The rudders on fins I and III

This view of the base of the A-4 exhibited in the National Air and Space Museum shows two jet vanes and the housings over the chainwheel for the air rudder (S.I. Negative #79-13219-12).

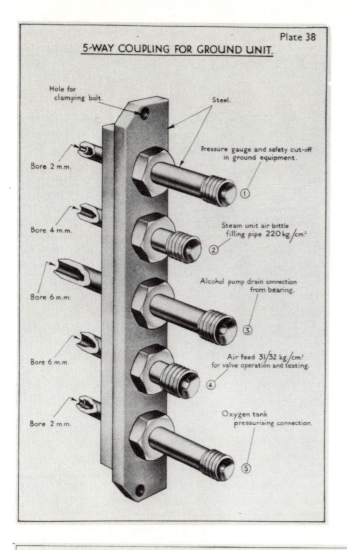

Plate 38

5-WAY COUPLING FOR GROUND UNIT.

Hole for clamping bolt.

Steel.

Bore 2 m.m.

Pressure gauge and safety cut-off in ground equipment.
①

Bore 4 m.m.

Steam unit air bottle filling pipe 220 kg./cm²
②

Bore 6 m.m.

Alcohol pump drain connection from bearing.
③

Bore 6 m.m.

Air feed 31/32 kg./cm² for valve operation and testing.
④

Bore 2 m.m.

Oxygen tank pressurising connection.
⑤

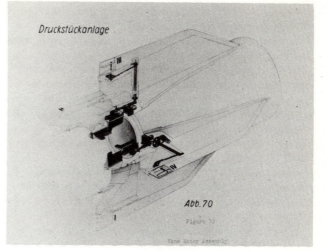

Druckstückanlage

Abb. 70

Figure 70

Vane Motor Assembly

Cutaway of the tail unit showing the drive mechanisms for the jet vanes and air rudders (S.I. Negative #79-12322).

The five-way coupling, located near the base of the rocket between fins II and III (S.I. Negative #79-13178).

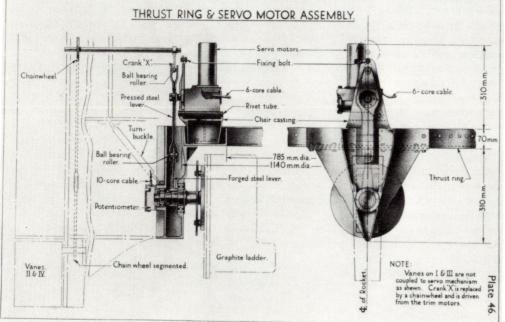

THRUST RING & SERVO MOTOR ASSEMBLY.

Chainwheel

Crank 'X'

Ball bearing roller.

Pressed steel lever.

Turn-buckle.

Ball bearing roller.

10-core cable.

Potentiometer.

Vanes. II & IV.

Chain wheel segmented.

Servo motors

Fixing bolt.

6-core cable.

Rivet tube.

Chair casting.

785 m.m.dia.
1140 m.m. dia.

Forged steel lever.

Graphite ladder.

6-core cable.

510 mm

70 mm

Thrust ring.

301 mm

Ç of Rocket.

NOTE:
Vanes on I & III are not coupled to servo mechanism as shewn. Crank 'X' is replaced by a chainwheel and is driven from the trim motors.

Plate 46

Servo motors powered the jet vanes (S.I. Negative #79-13191).

were not connected to the pitch vanes, but were driven by separate trim motors. These rudders were brought into operation when the yaw and roll rudders were out of synchronization to correct any unwanted rolling motion.

The jet vanes were made of graphite, as this material offered the best combination of desired characteristics: i.e., resistance to high temperatures, cost, availability, and ease of manufacture. Jet vanes allowed the rocket to be controlled from the instant of liftoff up to the time that sufficient velocity had been attained for the fins and rudders to function effectively.

The graphite vanes were manufactured by Siemans Planiawerke, which had plants at Berlin-Lichtenberg and Meitingen, near Augsburg. The materials and techniques used in the manufacture of the vanes were similar to those used for high-quality graphite electrodes.

Blanks for the vanes were made in the Lichtenberg plant, then shipped to the Meitingen facility for graphitizing. The blanks were then machined to shape. Special machines were used for this step. Half of the final machining was subcontracted to a machining firm called Faguswerke in Alfeld, near Hannover.

The blanks were made from the finest available petroleum and pitch cokes. After being mixed with a binder, the mixture was stamped into a horizontal extrusion press. After extrusion, the blanks were baked at 1150° C in a ring furnace. Following baking, the blanks were X-rayed to check for internal flaws. Only about 50 percent of the blanks were approved for further processing. The blanks were then pitch-treated, baked a second time, again pitch-treated, then baked for a third and final time.

These blanks were then shipped to Meitingen for electrode graphitization and machining either there or at Faguswerke. The blanks were first sawn to rough shape, then finished on a "milling-copying" machine which could machine two blanks at a time. It was specially developed for this task and used a master cam template and tungsten carbide milling cutters. After machining, the vanes were placed in a drying oven for one hour. To guard against the absorption of moisture, the vanes were sprayed with lacquer. As a final quality-control measure, the finished jet vanes were strength-tested on a machine in which hydraulic rams applied a force of 2200 pounds against the top of each vane.

Four jet vanes were needed for one rocket, but they were packaged in sets of five to allow for breakage during rocket assembly and handling.

Hydraulic servo motors powered the jet vanes. The motor assembly consisted of two identical pumps, an electric motor, valves, an electromagnetic relay, and an operating cylinder. The pumps were submerged in the oil reservoir. Each pump had two branches on its delivery side. One branch delivered oil to one side of the piston, the other back to the reservoir. The operating valves for the motor were on the branches leading back to the reservoir. By closing one of the valves, the pressure on the cylinder on that side was greater than that on the other, so the piston would move.

The piston was connected to the output shaft by a rod and bell crank. Movement of the piston caused the output shaft to rotate. The entire assembly was arranged such that the total travel of piston in the cylinder, which amounted to 55 mm, caused the output shaft to rotate 90°. By controlling which valve was closed, the direction of rotation could be controlled. The only positions where the piston could stop were neutral or at a 180° deflection. Any intermediate positions could be maintained only briefly, with the only control being over the rate and direction of rotation. The servo motors were not designed specifically for the A-4, but were adapted from those used on aircraft.

Two potentiometers were fitted with each jet vane, the pair being housed in a common case. One of the potentiometers was used to indicate the positions of the vanes during ground tests. The other was used during flight to determine whether or not the vanes were synchronized.

The fins were built from a sheet steel skin fastened to a framework of longerons and ribs. Lengthwise stiffening was accomplished by the two longerons. The outlet longeron had a boxlike reinforcement at its lower end that supported the A-4 when it was in the upright position. Each fin was further stiffened by 14 U-shaped ribs. Aerodynamic fairings smoothed the joints between the fins and the boat tail to reduce drag. A switch that started the timer in the control compartment when the rocket lifted off was built into fin I.

Three types of antennae were used for A-4 radio equipment. The lower section of the fins was made of a plastic material. On the mass-produced A-4s, the lower edge of the plastic part was framed with copper or cadmium-plated material. This strip antenna, or Schleifen antenna, on fins II and IV was about 80 cm long and was used for the radio control cutoff receiver. Two dipole antennae (Stab antennae) extended from conical housings built into the plastic portions of fins II and IV. These antennae were about 40 cm long and received signals from the guidance-beam transmitter (Hawaii) located on the ground.

A third type of antenna, called the Tur antenna, was built into the doors covering quadrants II and IV of the control compartment. These antennae were used for both reception and transmission for the radio control cutoff equipment. The two antenna plates were 180° out of phase, which gave the same results as using a horizontal dipole. By the end of the war, efforts were being made to use the Tur antenna for all radio transmission and reception, which would have eliminated the need for antennae in the tail section.

Four semiconical housings, one between each pair of fins, were located near the base of the boat tail. The housings between fins I and II and fins III and IV were for the turbo-pump exhaust. The oxygen tank topping-off inlet was located at the base of the housing between fins I and IV, while a five-way coupling was located between fins II and III. The coupling was used for servicing the A-4 prior to launch. It had connections for controlling the liquid oxygen tank pressure (2 connections), filling the P-battery in the steam generator, draining alcohol from the fuel pump, and providing pressurization to test the missile's pneumatic valves.

The tail unit weighed 750 kilograms (1650 pounds).

Appendix 2:
The V-2 In The National Air and Space Museum

The V-2 exhibited in the National Air and Space Museum was assembled using components from several rockets collected over a twenty-five year period.

After World War II, General H.H. "Hap" Arnold directed that outstanding examples of aircraft and related material be placed in storage at the former Douglas DC-4 Aircraft Plant at Park Ridge, Illinois. This collection, which contained over 100 aircraft and a somewhat battered V-2, was transferred to the Smithsonian Institution's National Air Museum on 1 May 1949. The missile had a sheet-metal cone for a warhead and was missing several tail unit components. The build-up for the Korean War in 1951 necessitated that aircraft production be resumed at Park Ridge, so the museum's collection was transferred to the recently acquired storage site at Silver Hill, Maryland.

Twenty-five years after it was added to the national collection, the V-2 was earmarked for restoration and exhibition in the new NASM building, scheduled to open during the American Bicentennial celebration. A survey of the missile revealed that it was missing the warhead, thrust ring and servo-motor assembly, graphite jet vanes, all control compartment components, rudders, and the aft antenna sections of all four fins. F.C. Durant, III, then the Assistant Director for Astronautics, searched for V-2 components in the United States, Great Britain, Germany, and the Netherlands.

A missile and a field launch platform were located at the NASA's George C. Marshall Space Flight Center (MSFC) in Huntsville, Alabama. They were transferred to the NASM in 1975. The V-2 had badly deteriorated, but did contain some of the components needed to complete the unit undergoing restoration at Silver Hill.

Dr. John Tanner, Director of the Royal Air Force Museum in Hendon, England, indicated that the RAF had a thrust ring assembly complete with servo-motors and graphite (jet deflector) vanes. The complete assembly was donated to the museum and flown by the RAF from Cosford, England, to the United States.

By the middle of December 1975, all the necessary parts to assemble the V-2 were on hand at the NASM Preservation and Restoration Facility. NASM aircraft restorers Charles Parmley, Richard Horigan, Dale Bucy, and Wilford Powell, began the task. Although the primary work performed at Silver Hill is aircraft restoration, many of the techniques applied equally well to refurbishment of the V-2. First, selection was made of the components to be used in assembly of the finished missile. The steel body halves were sand-blasted to remove old paint and rust. After cleaning them to bare metal, Wilford Powell chemically treated each component to deter future corrosion. The outer edges of the fins had been damaged and had to be replaced. The propulsion unit was disassembled, cleaned, treated, and rebuilt for placement in the rocket. The propellant tanks were omitted to reduce the weight supported by the fins. It was decided to paint the rocket in the black and white pattern used on the first successful round on 3 October 1945.

On 28 May 1976, after some 2000 man-hours of restoration work, the finished rocket was delivered to the museum. This was the last major space-related artifact to be placed in the building before it opened to the public on July 1. The V-2 was placed on the launch platform, which had also been cleaned and repainted by the Silver Hill restoration team. The V-2 is exhibited in the Space Hall, Gallery Number 114, in the museum.

In 1948 the Smithsonian Institution acquired a collection from the U.S. Air force that included over 100 aircraft and a somewhat battered V-2. This is how the missile appeared when it was added to the National Collection (S.I. Negative #79-13474).

After over 2000 man-hours of work, the V-2 was ready for exhibition in the National Air and Space Museum in 1976. The warhead and several other components came from another specimen received from the George C. Marshall Space Flight Center in 1975. The paint scheme is patterned after that of the first successful A-4, which was flown on 3 October 1942 (S.I. Negative #79-13219-2).

The thrust ring assembly, complete with jet vanes, potentiometers, and servo motors, was donated by the Royal Air Force (S.I. Negative #79-13219-7).

The V-2 in flight (S.I. Negative #80-4144).

A section of skin was omitted from one of the fins to allow the chain and sprocket drive for the air rudders to be seen (S.I. Negative #79-13219-4).

Appendix 3:
A-4 Missile Statistics

1. Weight of missile and components
   a. Warhead — 1000 kg
   b. Control Compartment — 480 kg
   c. Midsection — 742 kg
   d. Propulsion Unit — 931 kg
   e. Tail Unit — 750 kg
   f. Miscellaneous — 105 kg
   Total weight (dry) — 4008 kg
   Total weight, fully fueled — 12,700–12,900 kg
2. Overall length — 14,036 mm
3. Body diameter — 1,651 mm
4. Fin span — 3,564 mm
5. Combustion chamber pressure — 14.5 atmospheres
6. Temperature in combustion chamber — 2000° C
7. Exhaust velocity — 2000 m/s
8. Thrust — 252,000 newtons
9. Range — 300 km
10. Altitude at thrust termination — 28 km
11. Angle of trajectory at thrust termination — 78°
12. Maximum altitude on operational flights — 80 km
13. Velocity at thrust termination — 1500 m/s
14. Thrust duration — 60–63
15. Acceleration at liftoff — 1 g (9.8 m/s^2)
16. Acceleration at thrust termination — 6 g
17. Flight duration — ~ 320 s
18. Velocity at impact — ~ 800 m/s

Source: *Das Gerat A-4, Baureihe B.*

Bibliography

Armstrong, Clare H., et al. *V-2 Rocket Attacks and Defense*. United States Forces, European Theater, Antiaircraft Artillery Section, Study No. 42, File No. R 471.6/1, N.D. [ca. 1946].

AVKO (Altenwalde Versuchs Kommando). *Die Fernrakete* [*The Long Range Rocket*]. Document prepared by German personnel working on Operation Backfire, 1945.

Bilek, V.H., and McPhilimy, J.D. *Production and Disposition of German A-4 (V-2) Rockets (Project No. XT-1)*. Headquarters Air Materiel Command, Wright Field, Dayton, Ohio: Staff Study No. A-SS-2167-ND, 1948.

Cooksley, Peter G. *Flying Bomb*. New York: Charles Scribner & Sons, 1979.

Davis, Brian L. *German Army Uniforms and Insignia 1933–1945*. New York: World Publishing Company, 1972.

Dawson, P.J. *German Organisation and Personalities Engaged in Research and Development of Armaments During the Second World War* [sic]. Ministry of Supply, London, Report No. 436/I, 1948.

Delsasso, L.A., deBey, L.G., and Reuyl, D. *Full-Scale Free-Flight Ballistic Measurements of Guided Missiles*. Ballistic Research Laboratories Report #660, Aberdeen Proving Ground, Maryland; January 1948.

Dornberger, Walter. "The Lessons of Peenemünde." Technical Intelligence Branch, OWC, GU-15, 460, N.D. [ca. 1958].

Dornberger, Walter. *V-2*. New York: Viking Press, 1958.

Emme, Eugene M., *Aeronautics and Astronautics, An American Chronology of Science and Technology in the Exploration of Space 1915–1960*, U.S. Government Printing Office, 1961.

Eyestone, S.F., *A Study of the German Type II Accelerometer*, Report #AL-123, Los Angeles: North American Aviation, Inc., 1947.

Fedden, Roy. *The Fedden Mission to Germany*. Combined Intelligence Objectives Sub-Committee, London, 1945.

Felkin, S.D. *The A-4 Rocket—Further Information*, A.D.I. (K) Report No. 228/1945, March 1945.

Felkin, S.D. *More Information on the A-4 Rocket*, A.D.I. (K) Report No. 34B/1945, 7 Jan 1945.

Fogel, H.M. *Fuzing System of German A-4 Rocket (V-2)*, Combined Intelligence Objectives Sub-Committee, G-2 Division, SHAEF, Items No. 3 and 4, File No. XXVII-37, April 1945.

Fraser, L.W., and Siegler, E.H. *High Altitude Research Using the V-2 Rocket, March 1946–April 1947*, Bumblebee Series Report #81, The Johns Hopkins University, Applied Physics Laboratory, Silver Spring, Maryland, July 1948.

Friedman, Henry. *Summary Report on A-4 Control and Stability*. Headquarters Air Materiel Command, Wright Field, Dayton, Ohio, Report #F-SU-2152-ND, 1947.

Garlinski, Josef. *Hitler's Last Weapons*. New York Times Books, New York, 1978.

Garstens, M.A., Newell, H.E., Jr., and Siry, J.W. *Upper Atmosphere Research Report Number I*. Naval Research Laboratory Report No. R-2955, Office of Naval Research, Washington, D.C., 1 October 1946.

Gatland, Kenneth. *Missiles and Rockets*. New York: Macmillan Publishing Co., 1975.

German Long-Range Rocket Projectile-Storage and Launching Sites. A.I. 2(g) Report No. 4/x, 9 August 1944.

Hanrahan, James S., and Bushnell, David. *Space Biology*. New York: Basic Books, Inc., 1960.

Hargest, W.J. "Assembly Technique on V-2 Bombs Revealed in Underground Factory." *American Machinist*, 16 August 1945.

Helfers, M.C. *The Employment of V-Weapons by the Germans During World War II*. Office of the Chief of Military History, U.S. Army, Washington, D.C. 31 May 1954.

Huzel, Dieter. *Peenemünde to Canaveral*. Englewood Cliffs, New Jersey: Prentice-Hall, Inc., 1962.

Interim Report on Large Sites, Rocket Firing Platforms and Rocket Storage Sites in the Pas de Cal-
ais Area. A.I. 2. (L) Report No. 114, 7 October 1944.

Irving, David. *The Mare's Nest.* Boston: Little Brown and Company, 1965.

Kay, Anthony L. *Buzz Bomb.* Monogram Close-Up 4, Boylston, Massachusetts: Monogram Aviation Publications, 1977.

Klee, Ernst, and Otto Merk. *The Birth of the Missile.* New York: E.P. Dutton & Co., 1965.

Kooy, J.M.J., and Uytenbogaart, J.W.H. *Ballistics of the Future.* Haarlem, Holland: The Technical Publishing Company H. Stam, 1946.

Lasby, Clarence G. *Project Paperclip.* New York: Ateneum, 1971.

Ley, Willy. *Rockets, Missiles, and Men in Space.* New York: Viking Press, 1968.

Martenson, C.D. *Operations "Backfire" and "Clitterhouse" (British Firing of V-2 Rockets).* Military Attache, London, Report R 5499-45, 1945.

Michel, Jean. *Dora.* New York: Holt, Rinehart, and Winston, New Yoirk, 1979.

Mossop, I.A. *The Electrolytic Integrating Accelerometer for the Automatic Control of Range of*
the German A-4 Rocket. Royal Aircraft Establishment, Farnborough Hants, R.A.E. Report
EL.1387, 1946.

Munson, Kenneth G. *Aircraft of World War Two.* London: Ian Allan, Ltd., 1962.

Newell, H.E., Jr., and Siry, J.W. *Upper Atmosphere Research Report Number II.* Naval Research
Laboratory Report No. R-3030, Office of Naval Research, Washington, D.C. 30 December
1946.

New York Times, "V-2 Assembly Plant is Found in Mountain," 14 April 1945.

Prosecution Brief, Nordhausen War Crimes Trial. National Archives Microfilm Publication M-
1079.

Oberkommando des Heeres [High Command of the Army]. *Das Gerät A-4, Baureihe B,* [*The*
Assembly A-4, Model B], 2 January 1945. (Translated by the General Electric Company,
Schenectady, N.Y.).

Ordway, Frederick I., and Sharpe, Mitchell R. *The Rocket Team.* New York: Thomas Y. Crowell,
1979.

Schulze, H.A. *Technical Data on the Development of the A-4 (V-2).* George C. Marshall Space
Flight Center, Huntsville, Alabama, 1965.

Speer, Albert. *Inside the Third Reich.* New York: The Macmillan Company, 1970.

Squadron History, 13th Photo Reconnaissance Squadron, 7th Photo Reconnaissance Group. 1
October–1 November 1944. U.S. Air Force Historical Research Center, Maxwell Air Force
Base.

Storage and Launching of German Long-Range A-4 Rocket Projectile, A.I. 2(g) Report No. 6/x, 25
August 1944.

United States Army Ordnance Corps and the General Electric Company. *Hermes Guided Missile*
Research and Development Project 1944–1954. Technical Liaison Branch, Chief of Army
Ordnance, 25 September 1959.

United States Strategic Bombing Survey, Aircraft Division Industry Report. *Strategic Bombing of*
the German Aircraft Industry. Chapter IX, "Report on V-Weapon Production," 1945.

United States Strategic Bombing Survey, Military Analysis Division. *V-Weapons (Crossbow) Cam-*
paign. January 1947.

United States Strategic Bombing Survey, Physical Damage Division. *V-Weapons in London.* January 1947.

United States War Department. *Handbook on Guided Missiles of Germany and Japan.* Washington, D.C., 1946.

von Braun, Wernher. "German Rocketry," *The Coming of the Space Age.* Edited by Arthur C.
Clarke, New York: Meredith Press, 1967.

War Office. *Report on Operation Backfire*. London: Ministry of Supply, 1946.

White, L.D. *Final Report, Project Hermes V-2 Missile Program*. General Electric Co., Schenectady, N.Y. Report #R52A0510, 1952.

Wikle, Hugh H., and Steiner, Walter A. *Survey of Graphite Rudders for V-2 Rockets*. Joint Intelligence Objectives Agency, Washington, D.C., FIAT Final Report No. 105, 1945.

Winter, Frank H. "Birth of the VfR: The Start of Modern Astronautics." *Spaceflight,* Vol. 19 (1977), Nos. 7–8 (July–August).

GREGORY P. KENNEDY has been with the National Air and
Space Museum since 1971. He has extensive experience
in preparing exhibits in rocketry and space flight, and has
professional responsibility for the Museum's collection of
guided missiles, which includes German V-weapons. He is
co-author of the popular *Space Shuttle Operator's Manual*,
and has published widely on rocketry and space travel. He
is an officer in the Maryland Army National Guard, and
resides in Baltimore.